The Open University

A219 Exploring the Classical World

Block 3
The Roman Republic

Colin Andrews, Trevor Fear and Phil Perkins

This publication forms part of an Open University course A219 *Exploring the Classical World*. Details of this and other Open University courses can be obtained from the Student Registration and Enquiry Service, The Open University, PO Box 197, Milton Keynes, MK7 6BJ, United Kingdom: tel. +44 (0)870 333 4340, email general-enquiries@open.ac.uk

Alternatively, you may visit the Open University website at http://www.open.ac.uk where you can learn more about the wide range of courses and packs offered at all levels by The Open University.

To purchase a selection of Open University course materials visit http://www.ouw.co.uk, or contact Open University Worldwide, Michael Young Building, Walton Hall, Milton Keynes MK7 6AA, United Kingdom for a brochure. tel. +44 (0)1908 858785; fax +44 (0)1908 858787; email ouwenq@open.ac.uk

The Open University
Walton Hall, Milton Keynes
MK7 6AA

First published 2006.

Edited and designed by The Open University.

Typeset by The Open University.

Printed in the United Kingdom by TJ International Ltd, Padstow.

ISBN 0 7492 9650 X

1.2

B/a219_b3_e1i2_074929650X

The paper used in this publication contains pulp sourced from forests independently certified to the Forest Stewardship Council (FSC) principles and criteria. Chain of custody certification allows the pulp from these forests to be tracked to the end use (see www.fsc-uk.org).

CONTENTS

Front cover photo by Phil Perkins

Introduction to Block 3

Block timetable

This block comprises seven weeks' work: that is, six study weeks and a final week to write TMA 04 (where you will be required to comment on a short text or image and write an essay). The block is divided into an introductory part, four main parts and a short sixth concluding part. Each part enables you to study different aspects of the Roman republic and its people. They are:

1   **Greek colonies and the peoples of Italy and Rome**. A brief discussion of Greek colonies in Italy, with a case study of the city of Poseidonia, followed by work on the cultural relationship between Greece and Rome.

2   **The political system in the late republic.** A study of the political system of the Roman republic.

3   **Building history: ancestors, achievements and children**. An analysis of the competing individuals and dynasties that ruled in the city of Rome.

4   **Land, people and power**. A study of how the Roman republican system collapsed and a new political system emerged.

5   **Poetry and Politics in Augustan Rome**. The relationship between Roman poetry and its cultural context.

6   **Conclusion to Block 3**. A short final part containing consolidation and revision.

You should try to keep to the timetable for this block as much as possible, to allow you to complete the TMA at the appropriate time. Your Study Calendar indicates how the work is divided up.

Aims and objectives

In Blocks 1 and 2 you have focused mainly on individual works: poems, plays, buildings and speeches have formed the anchors of your study. Here our approach changes and you will explore a historical theme rather than individual cultural artefacts. You will begin to draw together a range of sources for exploration, analysis and criticism, thereby developing a broader critical understanding of historical concepts. As you study you will gain knowledge about a different period and further improve your skills in using and analysing sources.

The main learning outcomes of this block are:

1   To acquire and develop the skills needed for working with and understanding historical and poetic sources.

2   To enable you to engage with a scholarly publication and critically analyse its content and argument.

3   Through critical and close reading, to bring ideas and information drawn from a wide variety of sources to bear on historical and cultural questions.

4   To gain an overview of the political and cultural world of republican Rome, and to explore the relationship between literature and its political, social and cultural context.

Materials required

To study this block you will need:

- *The Oxford Companion to Classical Civilization* (*OCCC*)

- *Rome in the Late Republic* (Beard and Crawford)

- Book of Essays: *Experiencing the Classical World* (*ECW*)

- Readings Book 2

- Illustrations Book

- Audio-Visual Notes 2

- Assignment Book

- CD4, 'Poetic voices, political worlds'

- DVD3, Section 1, 'The city of Paestum'; Section 2, 'Seianti: an Etruscan noblewoman'; Section 3, 'The *Campus Martius*'; Section 4, 'The Roman forum'

- Course website ('ICT': timeline, pronunciation guide, online maps; 'Course links Block 3')

General orientation

The first part of Block 3 is a link between the Greek world you have studied in Blocks 1 and 2 and the study of the cultural and political development of Italy and Rome. It will not attempt to fill the gap but will sketch some of the connections between Greece and Rome, and also familiarise you with the geography of Italy and the chronology of the Roman period.

In the following four parts of the block you will be exploring the rich and complex world of republican Rome. Rome expelled its kings and became a republic at the end of the sixth century BCE, and a system of government was established that persisted (though not without change) for nearly 500 years, until Augustus established himself as emperor and sole ruler of the Roman world. For the first half of this period evidence and sources are in short supply, but at the end of the period the quantity of surviving material is almost overwhelming, and it is possible to follow the daily ups and downs of political manoeuvrings, which combined to break down the old political system. You will be studying some aspects of that political breakdown in this block.

Furthermore, you will be placing the politics and constitution of the Roman republic in their social and cultural contexts, combining archaeology and art with history. Politics may be seen as one expression of how groups and individuals interact within society and you will be studying this, especially in relation to powerful families in Rome. Roman republican society existed in a rapidly expanding city that was not only a setting for action and activity, but also a constructed expression of social structures and cultural experiences. Throughout the block you will observe the interplay between individuals, their society and the world they built and occupied (see Plate 38 in the Illustrations Book). These studies are linked by the historical theme of the breakdown of the Roman republican political system, and this theme was constructed and analysed by Romans themselves as they actively constructed and wrote their own histories; something we still do today, when working from what has survived.

In this period there were no emperors; instead, Rome's citizens governed its increasingly large empire. Their political system, closely related to their military organisation, created an immensely competitive society. Social and political rivalry became manifest in political and personal antagonism. It also spilled over into both religion and culture as powerful individuals vied to display their relationships to the gods through the building of elaborate temples in the city. Our primary purpose will be to examine why this system ended in a series of bloody civil wars and was replaced by a form of one-man rule – effectively a monarchy. We won't be able to explore every episode in detail, but by concentrating on a few key moments I hope that you will gain a good sense of the tremendous changes that were taking place during this key period.

The block ends with a study of Roman literature and the voices of some particular Romans, poetically reflecting on their own politics, society and history. It picks up some of the strands from the second part of the block, and investigates how history and poetry intertwine to become instruments of social and cultural politics in the late republic and the Augustan period.

Part 1 Greek colonies, the peoples of Italy and Rome

1.1 Introduction

The Mediterranean world has never been clearly divided into 'east' and 'west' or 'Greek' and 'Roman'. At all times there will have been some form of contact between the different regions of the Mediterranean. But at the end of the eighth century BCE contacts started getting closer as the Greeks began both to trade with the indigenous people of Italy – particularly for bronze and iron – and also to settle, building new cities and taking land to farm. This phase of settling, or colonisation, went along with the spread (conscious or otherwise) of Greek culture, a process generally known as Hellenisation.

Throughout the remainder of the first millennium BCE these contacts developed and intensified. Hellenisation is a much debated phenomenon, and the term itself, meaning 'becoming Greek-like', brings with it two misleading ideas: first, that there was such a thing as 'Greek culture' at that time which could be transferred from Greeks to others; and secondly, that there was a cultural void where the Greeks arrived – that the peoples in Italy (in this case) had no pre-existing culture of their own and just soaked up Greek culture as if they were sponges. As ever, things were not quite that simple, and rather than thinking of Hellenisation as a single or one-way process, it is more exciting and challenging to see it as a multiplicity of strands of Greek culture interacting with other cultures elsewhere in the Mediterranean. You can find a discussion of Hellenism and Hellenisation in the *OCCC*, but the emphasis there is placed on the eastern Mediterranean, particularly in the time of Alexander the Great. Nevertheless, the general points made are equally applicable to Italy and Rome. In the remainder of this introductory part you will be introduced to some examples of Hellenisation, and it forms an underlying theme of your studies in the rest of Block 3. Although the block doesn't explicitly compare Rome with the aspects of Athens that you have studied in Block 2, it does provide a parallel example of a city and empire ruled by a belligerent and competitive élite, and some of the themes you have studied in Athens can also be found in Rome.

1.2 Greek colonies

One of the defining characteristics of the Mediterranean Classical world – both Greek and Roman – is that cities became a distinctive element of settlement patterns. Throughout the region the city, with its surrounding territory occupied by farms and villages, became the typical form of human settlement. You have already studied the important city of Athens and its relationship with the city of Sparta. But the Greek cities were not alone in the Mediterranean: cities with other cultural traditions were to be found in Italy, northern Africa, the Levant and Egypt well before the middle of the first millennium BCE. These cities, each with their own political, social and cultural organisation, did not exist in isolation. All were linked to one another by their proximity to the Mediterranean Sea: the sea, in the ancient world, was a connecting element rather than a barrier. And so although the cities were generally politically independent from one another, they were in constant contact, either formally connected by treaties, or related by blood, or informally by trade and cultural exchange. Plato famously likened the Greek cities of the eastern Mediterranean to 'frogs sitting around a pool' (*Phaedrus* 109b). The Greek cities shared cultural and structural elements that made them characteristically Greek, and Plato's simile suggests their willingness to take to the waters of the Mediterranean. The similarity of Greek cities around the Sea was partly due to a shared culture and history but also, more directly, to the phenomenon of Greek colonisation.

Exercise

Read the extract from Homer's *Odyssey* below and note down the actions of Nausithoös and the areas of life he influenced.

> So long-suffering great Odysseus slept in that place
> in an exhaustion of sleep and weariness, and now Athene
> went her way to the district and city of the Phaiakian
> men, who formerly lived in the spacious land, Hypereia,
> next to the Cyclopes, who were men too overbearing,
> and who had kept harrying them, being greater in strength.
>   From here
> godlike Nausithoös had removed and led a migration,
> and settled in Scheria, far away from men who eat bread,
> and driven a wall about the city, and built the houses,
> and made the temples of the gods, and allotted the holdings.
> But now he had submitted to his fate, and gone to Hades',
> and Alkinoös, learned in designs from the gods now ruled there.
> (Homer, *Odyssey* 6.1–12)

Discussion

Generally, Nausithoös acts as a caring protector, leading his people and developing structures for the city – defensive, domestic, religious and economic. He provides for their essential physical and spiritual needs while setting up a new city, complete with an organisation of the farm land in a remote place.

Exercise

Later in the same book Odysseus is taken to the city of the Phaeacians (or Phaiakians, as in Lattimore's translation). The city is described by the nymph Nausikaa, daughter of the ruler of the city, King Alkinoös. Read the description below and list the main physical elements of the settlement mentioned in the passage.

> 'Rise up now, stranger, to go to the city, so I can see you
> to the house of my own prudent father, where I am confident
> you will be made known to all the highest Phaiakians.
> Or rather, do it this way; you seem to me not to be thoughtless.
> While we are still among the fields and the lands that the people
> work, for that time follow the mules and the wagon, walking
> lightly along with the maids, and I will point the way to you.
> But when we come to the city, and around this is a towering
> wall, and a handsome harbor either side of the city,
> and a narrow causeway, and along the road there are oarswept
> ships drawn up, for they all have slips, one for each vessel;
> and there is the place of assembly, put together with quarried
> stone, and built around a fine precinct of Poseidon,
> and there they tend to all that gear that goes with the black ships,
> the hawsers and the sails, and there they fine down their
>   oarblades;
> for the Phaiakians have no concern with the bow and the quiver,
> but it is all masts and the oars of ships and the balanced vessels
> themselves, in which they delight in crossing over the gray sea ...'
> (Homer, *Odyssey* 6.255–72)

Discussion

Once again the settled countryside, the city walls and the temple are mentioned, but this extract also describes the stone-built meeting place of the people, the *agora*. The location of the city is also described: Nausikaa tells Odysseus about the harbours to each side of the city, how it is connected to the shore by a causeway, and a road where ships are drawn up and maintained.

The city is fictional of course, but nevertheless Homer describes the essential features of a Greek colonial city. Furthermore, it would seem he is describing urban features from his own time (eighth century BCE), particularly the temple precinct, since stone temples did not exist before this time – elsewhere in the *Odyssey* the gods are worshipped at open-air altars rather than temples. I'm sure that the problems of relating the poetry of Homer to specific historical evidence and periods will be familiar to you from your study of Block 1. Although Homer was not describing a specific city (as far as we know), some ancient historians do provide accounts of the circumstances of the founding of cities.

Thucydides and the colonisation of Sicily

Thucydides, whom you have already met in Block 2, is one such historian. He provided part of the background to the conflict between the cities of Athens and Sparta – the backdrop in fact to Aristophanes' *Lysistrata*. A part of that conflict was the attempted Athenian invasion of the island of Sicily in 416/5 BCE. As an introduction to telling that part of the history of the war, Thucydides wrote an account of the history of the island and its colonisation by various Greeks and others. You will be asked to read this passage shortly, but before you do, a few preparatory comments will help you to see its significance, famous in the ancient history of Greece and Italy.

The sequence of events in Thucydides' account, and the times given between each event, provide the raw material that has enabled historians to date and reconstruct the history of Greek colonisation in Sicily between the eighth and the seventh centuries BCE. This passage is the principal source of literary evidence for constructing a chronology of cultural development in the central Mediterranean. Where precisely Thucydides (writing towards the end of the fifth century BCE) got the information for his factual statements is not certain, but it is generally thought that he depended on a fifth-century Sicilian writer called Antiochus of Syracuse. There are a few references to the same events by later historians whose information in some cases supports the dates given by Thucydides, but in others contradicts them. There is no need for us to go into all the messy details here, but generally historians have chosen to believe that the dates provided by Thucydides are reliable, even though they are not provable.

Archaeological discoveries made at the sites mentioned by Thucydides provide some back-up for the dates he gives, in that they have yielded pottery that is consistent with the dates given by Thucydides, but there is a danger of creating a rather circular argument here. If pottery is found at a site dated in Thucydides' account, it is possible to date the earliest pottery from that site to the date provided by Thucydides. The same type of pottery can then be used to confirm the date of another site mentioned by Thucydides as being founded at the same time. The circularity of the argument is clear enough in this case, but when the chain of connections between sites, finds and dates becomes more complex, it becomes difficult to disentangle their interdependence and ultimate reliance on uncertain dates. Apart from the problem of logic, the finding of a particular type of pottery in itself is not necessarily indicative of the founding of a colonial city. Instead, the pottery may have arrived through trading networks, or casual contacts between Greeks and indigenous people in the areas where Greek colonies were later founded, and so pottery alone does not provide evidence for the founding of a city.

I hope that this rather technical preamble has illustrated that dates themselves are not necessarily as certain and reliable as they might appear to be.

Exercise

Read Thucydides' account of the history of Sicily in Reading 3.1 of Readings Book 2. As you read, jot down some notes on the kinds of information that Thucydides is providing, and think about where or how he might have obtained this information. Aim to **analyse** and **categorise** rather than simply writing down the names, places and years – you are not expected to memorise them.

Discussion

As I mentioned in my preamble, Thucydides' sources are not known for sure, but the nature of some elements of his account should give you pause for thought. The Laestrygones and Cyclopes are said to be spoken of – implying some sort of independent testimony or perhaps body of common knowledge about them – but then Thucydides refers the reader to the poets for more information. The first poet that springs to mind is Homer: both the Laestrygones and the Cyclopes appear in the *Odyssey*. Thucydides' engagement of the reader with a reference to other authorities hardly provides evidence of reliability for the story; but what it does do, more importantly, is create the impression that Thucydides is at least being honest about the limitations of his own knowledge (and incidentally illustrates the importance of Homer as a historical source for writers of the fifth century BCE).

But we should also note that Thucydides is not as candid when it comes to other unsupported assertions; for example, in 6.2 'the facts show', but we are not told what the facts are – later it emerges that he is writing about a vague time in the past before the Trojan War. The desire to link history back to the Trojan War is clearly demonstrated by the assertion that the Elymi (2.1.3) were refugees from Troy. All of the history provided here for early Sicily and Italy has no known basis in verifiable fact; for example, the people known as the Elymians, from the archaeological remains of their culture, display absolutely no characteristics that can be related to the archaeological remains of Troy. However, as Thucydides gives us the *impression* of recounting established facts, presumably he is telling a traditional account of the prehistory of Sicily rather than just making up a story as he moves from mythological to non-Greek to Greek settlers.

Yet it is striking that his way of telling the prehistory of Sicily is remarkably similar to the history of the Greek colonisation of the island, with movements of peoples and seaborne adventures and battles between competing groups. The latter part of the passage, where Thucydides describes the Hellenic settlements, is a breathless account that is unified by its constant recounting of the names of the individuals who led the colonists, the names of the cities they came from, the places they went to and the struggles they faced. From time to time this cataloguing of the colonies contains mention of some geographical or topographical features, and occasionally accounts of interaction with indigenous inhabitants of Sicily. The specific Greek language used by Thucydides indicates that he was referring to some other written accounts while composing these statements, possibly those of Antiochus of Syracuse; but, as we know, his sources are uncertain.

I would also say that an element of the context of Thucydides' account intrudes here, for Syracuse and Gela were both allies of Sparta, and Leontini an ally of Athens. The rivalry between the two Greek cities in the colonial past prefigures their later conflict, which is, of course, the subject of Thucydides' history. You have already come across specific aspects of this context when you studied the debate in the Athenian Assembly in Essay Five of *Experiencing the Classical World*.

Chronology

This account is the most important written source for establishing the chronology of Greek colonisation. Don't worry though: you are not about to be asked to memorise all the names and dates, just to understand the general points being made. All of the dates provided hang from the date of the destruction of Megara Hyblaea, which can be dated independently to 483 BCE. From this date it is possible to work out a date of foundation for most of the other places named, starting with Naxos in 734 BCE. These dates are not necessarily certain, and some are contradicted by other written sources, but they do more or less coincide with the dates provided by the pottery finds from the Sicilian sites. What is more, some of the intervals of time between foundations fall close to 35 years, a conventional measure of a generation. This raises the possibility that Thucydides' source was counted in generations rather than years.

I've added the dates that can be worked out from the Thucydides' passage to a communal timeline called 'Sicily Chronology' which you can access from the course website. This has been prepared to provide you with an example of the kind of timelime that you can construct by extracting information from sources. You may notice that as the timeline works using exact dates, it is not very good at dealing with uncertainties such as 'about' or 'almost': you can record this kind of doubt as a comment. What strikes me when comparing the timelines for 'Homer and the Greek "Dark Age"' and 'Sicily Chronology' is that where they overlap, the dates of the Sicilian colonies are all very early and precise for such relatively firm dates when compared to the entries on the other timelines (which all tend to be of a rather general nature between 750 and 650 BCE). This observation underlines the fact that Greek contacts with the western Mediterranean are a feature of the very earliest recorded history of the Greeks.

If you'd like to know more, the *OCCC* provides further information under the entry for 'Sicily', and the entry for 'colonisation, Greek' will introduce you to the broader picture and geographical range of Greek colonisation.

Even if Thucydides' account of the colonisation of Sicily makes it sound like a simple process of the Greeks leading their people out to build new cities, the process was, of course, complex and multi-faceted – as is hinted at by the references to struggles and indigenous peoples. Traditionally, Greek colonisation has been seen as bringing civilisation to barbarian lands and spreading the benefits of Greek culture to areas previously unexposed to civilisation. Such explanations are often influenced by more recent colonial episodes involving western powers in the eighteenth, nineteenth and twentieth centuries. However, it is easy to suggest a *general* parallel between, say, the British colonising North America in the seventeenth century and the Greeks colonising the western Mediterranean between the eighth and the sixth centuries BCE, but it is much more difficult to sustain the parallel in any detailed discussion. In this section I'm not going to attempt to settle all the issues surrounding Greek colonisation, but I'm sure that your previous study of the relationships between Greeks and Persians, and Greeks and other Greeks, will have provided you with an awareness of inter-cultural dynamics in the Greek world.

You might be wondering why in a block introducing the Roman world you have, up to now, still been studying Greeks. I'll explain. Our knowledge of ancient history derives principally from ancient written sources that have survived to the present. Writing spread through the Aegean and Italy during the eighth and seventh centuries BCE, but the only fragments of written history of parts of Italy that have survived are Greek. These accounts – these Greek voices producing history – are only partial and there is no single complete surviving account of everything. If you think back to the account of Thucydides, it is told from a Greek point of view (the technique of focalisation). All of the earlier peoples of Sicily are described as immigrants from elsewhere and therefore any prior claims to land they might hold are diminished since they, like the Greek colonists, are incomers. Furthermore, the way the different cities competed in Sicily reflects their rivalries in Greece, and so to some extent the history of Sicily becomes an extension of the history of Greece. This is a result of the skill, art and rhetoric of Thucydides and is a consequence of the Greek context within which he is writing. As our historical knowledge of early Italy is mediated by Greek voices, our attempts at understanding and describing this history are therefore influenced by the 'priorities, practices and terminology' (*OCCC*, p.180) of Thucydides as well as our own. One way to overcome these obstacles is to consider, if possible, accounts of the same event by different authors, and this is an approach you will take later in the block in your study of the Roman republic (see Part 2). Another is to investigate consciously the other side of the story and attempt to develop an understanding of the colonised peoples, the ones who *didn't* write the surviving history, and we can do this by investigating archaeological and art historical sources. This will lead us eventually to Rome.

1.3   Case study: Poseidonia

I'd like you now to look at a case study of the city of Poseidonia (later renamed Paestum) which will provide you with an opportunity to study the archaeology of a Greek city in Italy, and to follow its history and development. Greek incomers built a city on the western shore of southern Italy, but they were settling on land already occupied by an indigenous people, the Lucanians, with whom they eventually came into conflict. The Lucanians did not write their own history, but it may be at least partially understood by studying their interaction with first the Greeks, and later the Romans, who conquered the Lucanians in the third century BCE as the Roman republic expanded and gradually conquered the whole of Italy.

Exercise

For a very brief account of the city, consult the *OCCC* entry for Paestum. Rather than simply making notes on the information contained there, I would like you to construct a **set of headings**, which you can use for gathering notes on topics related to the city.

Discussion

You will have noticed that the *OCCC* entry is fairly generalised. DVD3, Section 3 provides a more detailed account of how the city developed and the cultural influences it experienced, and you will need to take notes under the headings you've composed as you watch. At the end of the section you will be asked to compile your own *OCCC*-style entry for the city, derived from what you have learned.

Exercise

Now watch DVD3, Section 1 on the history and archaeology of the colony and city of Poseidonia. As you watch, take notes under the headings you collected from the *OCCC* entry for Paestum in the previous exercise. You may also find it helpful to have to hand Plates 36 and 37 in your Illustrations Book: an aerial view and a plan of the city.

Discussion

As you have seen, the DVD contains a rich variety of details on various topics related to the city. You will have picked up on the discussion of issues (such as the definition of Greek art and culture) that go beyond the city itself, and will also have considered how to interpret the evidence we have and how it may be used to discuss the cultural relations and development of southern Italy more generally.

Exercise

Now write your own *OCCC*-style entry for Paestum. Keep it brief, but plan it by noting the topics you think it should cover and then write a concise paragraph on the city.

You may be able to find more information on the internet – see 'Course links Block 3' on the course website for some starting points. A note of warning: be careful not to get distracted by the many tourist-oriented internet sites that do little more than provide superficial information and hotel details. Some additional ancient sources that you may find helpful are also supplied (see Readings 3.2 and 3).

Discussion

I am not going to provide you with a model answer here. Instead, compare your entry with the original *OCCC* entry. Do you think that your entry has a different emphasis? Have you concentrated more on the archaeology, the architecture or the history? Have you written more on the Greeks, the Lucanians or the Romans? Providing a balanced summary in a few words is challenging, but it is an essential skill when writing essay answers for TMAs, where you will often have to summarise complex evidence to support an argument or discussion, rather than set out all of the available information in great detail. It is also necessary for preparing good revision notes.

1.4   Etruscans and Greeks

The Etruscans were an indigenous people who inhabited much of central Italy, both to the north and south of Rome, where they neighboured the colony of Poseidonia and the Lucanians. They were literate and wrote in their own language, Etruscan, but unfortunately none of their own written history has survived. So inevitably we start once again with the Greeks, but, for a change, with a less than glorious episode from the history of Greek colonisation. This will provide us with another example of interaction between the Persians (or Medes) and the Greeks as well as a description of further interaction with the Etruscans.

Exercise

First of all, quickly read the entry for Herodotus in the *OCCC*, particularly Section 5 concerning 'reciprocity'. Then read the account, written by Herodotus, of the Phocaeans' failed attempt at colonisation (Reading 3.4). As you read, note down the themes in the passage, relating them to kinship and reciprocity where possible. (The events took place between *c.*545 and 540 BCE.)

Discussion

Here are my themes:

- Friendship and enmity between peoples/communities (Phocaeans, Carthaginians and Tyrrhenians); reciprocity.

- Religious duty (piety) seen in the founding of temples at Alalia.

- Poor reciprocity: friction with neighbours (Etruscans and Carthaginians gang up on the Phocaeans).

- More poor reciprocity: Etruscans kill prisoners and so are damned.

- Need to restore reciprocity: Etruscans seek divine guidance at Delphi.

- Stability achieved: Phocaeans go to Velia, capture the city and found their own settlement there.

This kind of analysis – looking for examples of reciprocity – particularly illustrates particularly how such a passage may be read both as an account of how and why the Phocaeans left Corsica and ended up in southern Italy, and also as a passage displaying forms of explanation that are characteristic of Herodotus' style. In the passage we also find evidence for interaction – in this case violent and warlike – between the Greeks and non-Greeks. The net result of the confrontation between the Phocaeans and the Tyrrhenians (Etruscans) was that there were no further attempts at Greek colonisation in Etruscan areas, and although the point is not emphasised by Herodotus, the Etruscans were clearly too strong for the Greeks to seize territory in areas they controlled.

Herodotus' account is the only surviving ancient source that mentions the Battle of Alalia, and one of only a few that concerns relationships between the Greeks and the Etruscans. Although the episode is only a minor skirmish in Greek history (it does not, for example, merit an entry in the *OCCC*), it takes on a much greater significance in terms of the history of the Etruscans because of its rarity as a historical source and the implications it has concerning Etruscan power and relationships with the Carthaginians. To gain a fuller understanding of conditions in early Italy it is necessary to rely on archaeological sources. If you read the *OCCC* entry on the Etruscans, you'll see that the range of the discussion goes beyond what is known from fragments of history. Their prehistoric predecessors, resources, material culture, trade and burial rites are all discussed, and the evidence for these comes not from the written word but from excavations in tombs and settlements. The author of the entry, David Ridgeway, suggests that the Hellenisation of the Etruscans was only a veneer (*OCCC*, p.269), but despite these reservations Greek influence was profound. No Greek cities were founded in Etruria, but there is some evidence for the presence of individual Greeks, from legendary sources as well as archaeological evidence: for example, the form of personal names and the Greek styles of locally-produced art (presumably made by Greek immigrants). Elements of Greek culture were adopted by some of the peoples of Italy: Greek gods such as Apollo and Hermes were adopted by the Etruscans and became *Apulu* and *Turms*. Other cases are more complex: the Etruscan *Tinia* becomes assimilated into the Greek Zeus and is often represented in a manner similar to the cult statue of Zeus at Olympia made by the sculptor Pheidias.

Yet I wouldn't consider it the case that the Etruscans took Greek art and religion wholesale; what seems more likely is that the Etruscans became familiar with Greek culture, selected certain elements from it and adapted it to meet their own needs. For example, the funeral of Patroclus (*Iliad*, Book 23, which you studied in Block 1, Section 3.5) appears to have been known to the Etruscans just as it was to the Lucanians (DVD3, Section 1, Track 3): certain Etruscan burials seem to reflect parts of the rituals, cremation and burial in an urn, burnt offerings, funeral games and so on. However, Etruscan burials do not directly copy the poetic descriptions of Homer; rather they share some common elements, as if both are drawing from a wider pool of cultural behaviour and adapting it to their own cultural and social needs.

This brief study of the Etruscans will, I hope, have given you a taste of some of the cultural complexity that was present in Italy during the Archaic and Classical periods. It has not been possible to go into much detail, but what should be clear is that Italy was fundamentally influenced by Greek settlers and the culture, society and political institutions they brought with them. What is more, it was not only in the areas of southern Italy where the Greek colonies were founded that Greek influence was felt, but also in places that were not colonised or ruled by Greeks, such as Etruria, or even Rome itself.

Between the areas of southern Italy settled by the Greeks, and the northern areas settled by the Etruscans, lay Rome, and the Romans were influenced by both Greece and Etruria. One account of early Roman history says that an Etruscan, Tarquinius Priscus, was King of Rome for a period, that he was descended from a Greek immigrant called Demeratus and that his great-grandsons later deposed the royal family and went on to be one of the founders of the Roman republic in 509 BCE. Of course, the reported history of this early period is not very reliable, and what truth there may be in it is thoroughly mixed up with myth and legend. Later on the Romans wrote histories of themselves that attempted to make a coherent narrative of their own early history, but as you will find out in this block, much of that history says more about the time that it was written than the time that it purports to describe. Archaeological excavations in Rome continue to find more and more evidence of the fascinating development of early Italy, but relating the finds to the written stories of Romulus founding the city, or the rule of Tarquinius Priscus, is far from straightforward, if not impossible. The most reliable modern account is provided by T.J. Cornell in *The Beginnings of Rome* (1995).

Although the following parts of this block will concentrate on the later Roman republic, a period when the historical sources are much more reliable and coherent, you will however be returning from time to time to the murky earlier history of Rome to explore how later generations of Romans exploited their own past.

1.5   Greek culture and Rome

Your work in this block so far will have made you realise that during the first millennium BCE, Italy not only possessed its own vibrant cultures but was also open to influences from elsewhere – particularly the Greek world. In this context Rome grew from being a small city ruled by kings to an empire stretching across the Mediterranean, governed by a political and cultural élite in Rome. In Parts 2 and 3 of the block you will be studying some aspects of this ruling élite and the city of Rome. We won't be presenting you with a detailed account of the foundation of the Roman republic, but if you would like to read that history there are some suggestions in the 'Further reading' section at the end of this part. You can also find some key topics covered in the *OCCC*.

Your set book, *Rome in the Late Republic*, referred to in this course as Beard and Crawford after its authors, is best seen as a series of essays on topics related to the late republic in Rome. You are not asked to sit down and read it from cover to cover; rather you are directed to read various pages at different points in the block. Some parts won't be set as reading, but they contain interesting and relevant discussion relating to the republic – even if they are not closely related to your learning in the block. The book also includes a detailed bibliography which you can use to pursue topics of particular interest in greater depth. Beard and Crawford was first published in 1985, then updated with an epilogue in 1999 which outlines how scholarship had progressed in the intervening years. Despite the fact that it was written over twenty years ago, the ideas in the book remain provocative and in some respects controversial. The topics it discusses are still hotly debated in contemporary scholarship and its strength lies more in the questions it poses, and those that it stimulates you to ask, than in the answers it might provide.

Exercise

To conclude this part and to become familiar with the set book, you should now read Beard and Crawford, Chapter Two, 'The Cultural Horizons of the Aristocracy', pp.12–24. This will introduce you to some of the key themes that we shall be pursuing in the rest of Block 3.

Discussion

I hope that reading this chapter has crystallised some of the issues that you been introduced to in this part of the block, as well as introduced the framework of cultural development which will provide the context for the topics you will be studying in more detail later in the block.

CMA 52

Now do CMA 52 in your Assignment Book. The CMA has been designed to enable you to assess your own learning during Blocks 1 and 2, as well as in this introductory part to Block 3. It focuses particularly on your understanding of concepts, as well as your ability to work with sources. Although it does not count towards your final grade, you must submit the CMA for marking: it will reassure you that you are progressing well and are prepared for Blocks 3 and 4.

References

Ancient sources

Homer, *The Odyssey*, in R. Lattimore (trans.) (1999) *The Odyssey of Homer*, New York: Harper Perennial.

Plato, *Phaedrus*, in R. Waterfield (trans.) (2002) *Plato: Phaedrus*, Oxford: Oxford University Press.

Thucydides, *The History of the Peloponnesian War*, in R. Crawley (trans.) (1997) *Thucydides: The History of the Peloponnesian War*, Ware: Wordsworth.

Modern scholarship

Cornell, T.J. (1995) *The Beginnings of Rome: Italy and Rome from the Bronze Age to the Punic Wars (c.1000–264 BC)*, London and New York: Routledge.

Further reading

Modern scholarship

Boardman, J. (1980) *The Greeks Overseas: Their Early Colonies and Trade* (3rd edn), London: Thames and Hudson.

Cornell, T.J. (1995) *The Beginnings of Rome: Italy and Rome from the Bronze Age to the Punic Wars (c.1000–264 BC)*, London and New York: Routledge.

Haynes, S. (2000) *Etruscan Civilization: A Cultural History*, London: British Museum Press.

Pedley, J.G. (1990) *Paestum: Greeks and Romans in Southern Italy*, London: Thames and Hudson.

Part 2 The political system in the late republic

2.1 Introduction

This part of the block aims to give you a basic understanding of the constitution of the Roman republic. Together we will attempt to identify and explore the main social and political problems which contributed to the collapse of the republican system and trace those key figures and events which help our understanding of how these problems and weaknesses evolved.

A further objective is to develop an understanding of how history is 'created'. We will continue our focus on ancient sources as preparation for the study of how they are used to create modern scholarship (as discussed in the Course Introduction) in Part 3. This should also help to develop your basic research skills, including the use of the internet.

The late Roman republic is particularly rich in ancient written sources. They are of a diverse range, including poetry, letters, history, biography, political and forensic speeches (i.e. a speech made in a court of law). But many are not contemporary with the events that they describe and all, without exception, were produced by élite males. Archaeological evidence is sparse but we shall be using it wherever possible to shed additional light on our discussions. Overall, I hope that this part of the block will communicate the richness of this period and will underline the necessity of using as wide a range of evidence as possible to deepen your understanding of the Classical world.

Historical background

Through conquests and alliances the Romans had emerged as the dominant power in Italy by the third century BCE. They were also acquiring significant power in the Mediterranean, which brought them into conflict with the Carthaginians (whom you met in Part 1 of this block). Carthage had originally been settled by the Phoenicians (hence 'Punic') perhaps as early as the ninth century BCE. During the next five centuries Carthage established a trading network over the western Mediterranean including southern Spain, Sardinia and Sicily, which the city jealously guarded. This eventually brought the Carthaginians into conflict with Rome, against whom they fought three wars. The First Punic War (264–241 BCE) resulted in the Romans acquiring their first overseas provinces: Sicily (241 BCE), Sardinia (238 BCE) and Corsica (227 BCE). The Second Punic War (218–201 BCE) against the Carthaginian Hannibal Barca was devastating. For more than a decade Hannibal roamed Italy defeating every Roman army sent against him. The Romans suffered such huge losses (perhaps as many as 50,000 in a single day at Cannae in 216 BCE) that they had to dig more deeply into their reserves of manpower than ever before. Eventually, victory gave Rome two new provinces in Spain in 197 BCE. When Rome embarked on the Third Punic War (149–146 BCE), Carthage presented no real threat to its interests, but the one-sided campaign ended with the utter destruction of Carthage; the city was demolished and the site cursed. This war resulted in Rome gaining another new province, Africa, in 146 BCE, which was in fact just a small part of the north African coastal strip, primarily modern Tunisia. In the same year Macedonia and Achaea were added to Rome's imperial portfolio.

This acquisition of empire had some important and far-reaching consequences for Roman society. Traditionally the Roman army had been recruited by the compulsory citizen service of men aged up to 46 and was primarily composed of small-scale peasant farmers. This was a common system in the ancient world and worked well enough when wars were seasonal, short and mainly local. But the Second Punic War swept this system away. Roman soldiers were increasingly called on to serve outside Italy for lengthy periods. Citizens probably had to serve for six years (technically for six campaigns) to discharge their responsibilities. They were poorly rewarded for their military service and six years spent away from their farms meant that many small farms became untenable and were sold to large landowners. So although poorer citizens did not benefit financially from the acquisition of empire, the élite did. Army officers and businessmen all managed to enrich themselves in this period. The gulf between rich and poor became wider than ever during the second century BCE, and the rich needed something to do with their money. They lavished it on their houses, with new forms of decoration such as mosaics and wall paintings appearing for the first time; they collected art, especially from the Greek world. They also bought land, the only respectable way for a member of the élite to hold and accumulate wealth. They staffed their new estates with slaves, which were for the first time cheap and plentiful as so many had been acquired as booty in Rome's wars.

Exercise

The first ancient source we shall look at is by Appian, who is our only surviving continuous narrative source for this period. Before you look at it, read the entry on Appian in the *OCCC* and make a few notes of those things you consider significant about his life and work. It is always important to know something about the context of ancient sources, in order to judge their usefulness in furthering your understanding of the period.

Discussion

I expect you will have noted that Appian was a Greek; not from Greece itself, but from Alexandria in Egypt, the famous centre of learning and culture. He was born around CE 100 and therefore is not a contemporary source for the period we are discussing. I hope you also noticed that Appian had a pretty interesting life, becoming a Roman citizen, moving to Rome and enjoying a successful career. We are told he became a *procurator* under the emperor Antoninus Pius who ruled between CE 138 and 161. If you were unsure what a *procurator* was, I hope that you looked it up to discover that a *procurator* was a civil administrator working directly for the emperor. Appian's only surviving work is part of a history of Rome from its beginnings: just eleven books have come down to us out of a probable total of 24. Remember when using ancient sources that it is important to analyse them for possible weaknesses. Might they be biased, for example? Are they contemporary? Who might they have been written or made for?

Exercise

Now read Appian 1.7 in Reading 3.5. As you read, consider the following questions:

- Which of the points made in my introductory paragraphs does Appian provide evidence for?

- Which new problems that are not mentioned above does he introduce?

Discussion

Appian discusses a number of the problems discussed earlier, such as how the rich increased the size of their estates, often by acquiring the land of small farmers. He also notes that slaves worked these large new estates. The reason he gives for this use of slave labour might have surprised you; it was not, Appian asserts, because slaves were cheaper but because they were not eligible for conscription into the army. He also introduces the notion of *ager publicus* or public land. This was basically land captured in war, much of which was confiscated from Italian tribes in the third century BCE. Some of it was used for planting colonies of Roman citizens, but it increasingly appears to have been appropriated by the élite because they could afford the investment required to make the land profitable. There was a law in force that limited the amount of public land any one person could acquire to 500 *iugera* (135 hectares), but it was not enforced and was universally ignored.

A further problem tied up with all this concerns the decreasing pool of Roman citizens eligible for military service. As already mentioned, the Roman army was a citizen army. The Romans did make use of their allies to fill the ranks, but these men were of varied non-citizen status and did not share in the decision-making processes. We shall have more to say about the complicated relationship between Rome and its allies a little later. Surprisingly, however, not all Roman citizens were eligible for military service – as we shall, see the very poorest citizens were prohibited from it.

The class system

Rome was a very wealth-conscious society. Citizens were divided into a number of classes on the basis of wealth, traditionally held as property. Every five years, two very senior magistrates would be elected, called censors. Their primary function was to hold a census of Roman citizens, recording how much wealth or property each individual owned. This would determine whereabouts in the rigid class system each person belonged. In Rome, your income and the value of your property were in the public domain and determined your position and role in society. The origins of this system are to be found in early Roman military organisation. The wealthier you were, the more equipment you could afford: the richest citizens, for example, could afford a horse, so they were *equites* or knights. Below them a man might be rich enough to afford a full panoply of armour and weapons and would join the ranks of the heavy infantry. Other citizens might only be able to afford a spear and shield and would be light-armed skirmishers.

At the top of Roman social ranking came the senatorial order. In this period you needed property worth 400,000 sesterces in order to qualify and your wealth had to be in land (a whole range of business activities were forbidden to senators) – a kind of landed aristocracy. Below them came the *equites* or knights, who also needed 400,000 sesterces to qualify – they were Rome's business class. There were then five property classes of citizens, and at the very bottom came citizens without property – the *proletarii* (named thus because they were considered too poor to contribute anything to the state except their children or *proles*). The *proletarii* were disqualified from military service because it was thought that those with no stake in society would be unreliable and should not have the privilege of defending it.

Originally, of course, they were disqualified because they could not afford to provide themselves with any weapons (although they had been called up and armed at the state's expense at times of severe crisis such as the war against Hannibal). The *proletarii* were, however, still citizens, and so held a formal status above that of many of Rome's allies, and slaves.

2.2   The constitution of the Roman republic

The constitution of the Roman republic is quite complicated and it's doubtful that many Romans fully understood all of its nuances. It was unwritten and had been in a continual state of evolution since the foundation of the republic, traditionally in 517 BCE. For the modern scholar there are not very many clear expressions of it in the surviving ancient literature. One of the best is by a historian named Polybius.

Like Appian, Polybius was Greek but was born three centuries earlier, around 200 BCE, into a family of prominent statesmen. He too became a politician and served as a *hipparch* (cavalry commander). After Rome's defeat of the Macedonian King Persius at the Battle of Pydna in 168 BCE, a thousand prominent Greeks were rounded up and sent to Italy as political detainees for an indefinite period – Polybius was among them. While in Rome Polybius became an extremely close friend of Scipio Aemilianus, a member of one of Rome's leading families and the son of Aemilius Paullus, the victor of Pydna. When the younger Scipio became leader of Rome's armies in his turn, Polybius accompanied him on campaigns, witnessing Scipio's destruction of Carthage in 146 BCE. Despite his experiences Polybius became an admirer of Rome and wrote glowingly about its achievements:

> There can surely be nobody so petty or so apathetic in his outlook that he has no desire to discover by what means and under what system of government the Romans succeeded in less than fifty-three years [220–167 BCE] in bringing under their rule almost the whole of the inhabited world, an achievement which is without parallel in human history.
>
> (Polybius, *The Rise of the Roman Empire* 1.1)

So now let's focus on that system of government which, according to Polybius, served Rome so well.

Exercise

Read Book 6.11 and 18 from Polybius' account of the republican constitution in Reading 3.6 (a) and (b). Identify the different elements of the constitution and how they each relate to one another.

- How would you characterise Polybius' view of the constitution?

- What sort of words might you use to describe it? (E.g. democracy? aristocracy? tyranny?)

- Where, in your view, does the real power reside?

Discussion

You probably noted that Polybius identifies three main elements in the republican constitution: **magistrates** (e.g. consuls), **senate** and **people**. You probably also noticed that there is a general air of approval. As far as Polybius is concerned, the Roman constitution is perfect: it is harmonious and balanced, the best of all political worlds. According to Polybius, it has democratic, aristocratic and monarchical elements. Despite this alleged harmony you may have felt that in the final part of the passage there is a suggestion of tensions within the system, as we are told that each must constantly keep the other two in check. Interestingly, Polybius further suggests that 'the people' are the most likely element to need curbing. Is this perhaps a clue about where real power resided?

Let's now look at these three elements in turn.

The three elements of the constitution

Magistrates

There was really only one 'career' open to an élite Roman male of the senatorial class and that was a public or political one. If a family had only one son, he would be expected to climb the *cursus honorum* (literally 'course of honour'), the name given by the Romans to the ascending ladder of magistracies, which culminated in the consulship. The *cursus* evolved over time with the constitution, but in its settled form an élite young man's career path was laid out for him. This was expensive and if a family had several sons only one might be able to embark on a public career. As you can see, the system was incredibly competitive.

Read the section entitled 'Magistrates' in Beard and Crawford, Chapter Four, 'Political Institutions', pp.52–55.

1   Make a list of magistracies and note down the ages at which they were generally held. How many of each type were there? How

long was each magistracy held for? Which magistracies were not compulsory?

2   Plot the career path of an average élite male born into the senatorial class, from the age of twenty onwards, and assume that he was enormously successful.

3   Consider the reasons why this system was so competitive. What effects might this have had on those seeking high office and on the political process in general?

Discussion

1   Your list probably looks something like this:

Quaestor	Age 30	20 posts	(after Sulla's reforms)
Tribune	Age 30	10 posts	
Aedile	Age 36	4 posts	
Praetor	Age 39+	8 posts	
Consul	Age 42	2 posts	

Each of these magistracies could only be held for one year and could generally only be held once. An ex-consul could seek re-election ten years after his first consulship, which in practical terms meant that one could normally only expect to hold high office once. You probably also noticed that only the quaestorship and praetorship are essential prerequisites for the position of consulship.

2   This list also plots out the career path of our élite young male, with the addition of several, usually ten, years of preliminary military service, which was compulsory. After the consulship it was usual to become the governor of a province with pro-consular *imperium* or power. One might also become a censor. Beard and Crawford aptly describe the system as a pyramid: it narrows the further up it you climb and there are always younger men at your heels. It was considered very important to achieve the appropriate office at the earliest permissible age.

3   Such intense competition had a range of effects. At one extreme there was political violence – one might simply kill or terrorise one's opponents. One might bribe the electorate (we will have more to say about elections when we look at the people's assemblies) and there is clear evidence that bribery became endemic in the later republican period. It is worth noting that no Roman magistrates were paid. One legitimate way of seducing the electorate was through the provision of games and other

entertainments. Men would bankrupt themselves in order to provide more lavish shows than their opponents. You can find out more about this phenomenon in Essay Nine of *Experiencing the Classical World*. Ultimately, the competitiveness of the system led to the most important men of the state fighting each other with their own loyal armies in order to achieve personal dominance.

Exercise

Now use the internet to find out the basic duties and areas of responsibility for each magistracy on the list. Your first port of call should be the A219 website where you will find some appropriate links ('Course links Block 3').

Discussion

Quaestor
Starting with the most junior post, quaestors were basically financial officers. They might serve with the legions or take up provincial posts.

Tribune
Tribunes chaired meetings of the people's assembly; they could introduce legislation and convene meetings of the senate. Possibly their most important power was the right to veto measures put forward by any other magistrate, even consuls.

Aedile
The aediles looked after the maintenance of public buildings; they oversaw supplies of food and fresh water. They also supervised markets and acted as trading standards officers. They were responsible for all the public games held during their year of office, organising the games themselves and paying most of the expenses from their own pockets. Even though this magistracy was not a necessary part of the *cursus*, the posts were sought-after as they enabled an aspiring politician to make a big splash before standing for the crucial praetorship.

Praetor
Praetors were primarily judges in the law courts and they administered justice generally. When the consuls were absent the praetors assumed their duties. After their year of office they might govern a province as a propraetor.

Consul
Consuls were the supreme magistrates of the state. They convened and presided over the senate, convened the assemblies

and introduced legislation; they also represented Rome in foreign affairs. Importantly they led Rome's armies: they were generals as well as politicians.

The senate

Exercise

Read Polybius 6.13 in Reading 3.6 (c). Make brief notes on the powers and responsibilities of the senate, for example, foreign affairs. Then jot down anything that the source *doesn't* tell us about the senate, but which you would like to know.

Discussion

You probably established that the senate had far-reaching powers and responsibilities. They had control over taxation and expenditure, were a court of law, and were also responsible for all aspects of foreign affairs including declarations of war. So far so good, but what would we like to know in addition to the information provided by Polybius? Perhaps, like me, you would like to know some of the more practical things, for example:

- How did one become a senator (e.g. by election)?
- How many were there in the senate?
- How often did they meet?
- Did they actually make law?

Exercise

Now read Beard and Crawford, Chapter Four, 'Political Institutions', pp.44–49 (up to the heading 'Assemblies') and pp.58–59 (the end of the chapter). See if you can find answers to some or all of the questions above.

Discussion

You should have been able to find answers to all four questions. Some are simple: for example, there were between 300 and 600 senators depending on the period and they met about 40 times a year.

The answer to the question on *how* one became a senator is a little more complicated. You probably gathered that there are several factors involved. First there is the property qualification: you have to be wealthy enough. Technically, you also have to be approved by the censors. But the most important qualification was your election to a junior magistracy, the quaestorship. So there was a sense in which senators were elected. In many ways the senate was a self-perpetuating body, but not entirely so. It is important to realise that the senatorial and equestrian orders were not mutually exclusive and compartmentalised. All senators began life as equestrians and the equestrian order 'fed' the senate. The senate is often described as permeable; the phenomenon of 'new men' or *novi homines* (singular: *novus homo*) demonstrates this. The term has two meanings: it might be applied to a man who merely becomes a senator (none of whose family has previously been members of the senate), but it is more commonly applied to men such as the Cato the Elder, Cicero and Marius, who not only became senators without the benefit of a senatorial background but rose to the highest office – the consulship. Such men were comparatively rare: only about fifteen are attested for the middle and later republican period.

In order to answer the question 'Did the senate make law?', it will be helpful to explore the third element of the constitution – the people.

The people

The role of the people in the republican constitution is at first glance important and influential. As Polybius writes: 'one could reasonably argue that the people have the greatest share of power in the government, and that the constitution is a democracy' (6.14). Let's examine this and see if Polybius' claim holds water.

Exercise

First read Polybius' account of the role of the people in the constitution in Reading 3.6 (d) which ends with the claim quoted above.

At this stage just note down which powers the people seem to have. Think about whether any of them overlap with the powers of the magistrates and senate we have already looked at. Once again, also think about what we are *not* told.

Discussion

Polybius emphasises the peoples' role as a court. They 'bestow offices', meaning that they elect magistrates; they also 'approve or reject' laws, another hugely important function. We might see in these functions elements of political systems that we are familiar with, and the Roman system could be seen as democratic, in the way that Polybius describes it at any rate.

I suspect, however, that it's the functions he glosses over which are more important. But what does he leave out? Well, he doesn't tell us anything about how the people were organised. For example, as you have already seen in Block 2, the adult male citizens of the Athenian constitution met in a body called the Assembly and voted on issues put before them. It was 'one man, one vote' and a simple majority carried the day. What Polybius rather disingenuously neglects to tell us is that in the Roman system there were two main peoples' assemblies (*comitia*), both with different functions and responsibilities – and in none of them was there a system of 'one man, one vote'. Instead, the Roman republic had the centuriate assembly (*comitia centuriata*) and the tribute or plebeian assembly (*comitia plebis tributa*), which was really two assemblies in one.

Its origins lie in the early days of the republic and the struggle between patricians and plebeians. Originally patrician families – a sort of closed group of aristocratic families – dominated the republic. Only they could be senators and magistrates and intermarriage between plebeians and patricians was forbidden. In order to try to gain equality with patricians, the plebeians (effectively all those who weren't patricians) set up their own assembly in the fifth century BCE (the *concilium plebis*) and elected their own magistrates (plebeian tribunes). Plebiscites, the laws passed by the *concilium plebis*, soon became binding on both patricians and plebeians and by about 300 BCE complete equality had been attained. The difference between a *comitia* and a *concilium* is that a *comitia* is (potentially at least) an assembly of all citizens, while a *concilium* is an assembly of only part of the citizenry: that is, an assembly restricted to plebeians, the *concilium plebis*.

By the period that concerns us, there was just one assembly attended by both patricians and plebeians. Technically, if the presiding magistrate was a plebeian tribune, the assembly was the *concilium plebis*, and if presided over by another magistrate, it was the *comitia tributa*, but there was no essential difference in its function or organisation. There was also a third assembly, the curiate assembly (*comitia curiata*) which by our period had limited functions: formally confirming the appointment of magistrates, overseeing the installation of priests, and making wills and adoptions.

Of the two main assemblies the centuriate assembly (*comitia centuriata*) was responsible primarily for electing important magistrates and the plebeian or tribal assembly (*comitia plebis tributa*), often called the 'peoples' assembly' was responsible for approving or rejecting laws put to them by magistrates. The centuriate assembly could also pass laws and was originally the primary legislative assembly, but the plebeian or tribal assembly eventually eclipsed it and by the end of the second century BCE almost all legislation was passed by the latter.

What is peculiar about both these assemblies is their method of voting. The names 'centuries' and 'tribes' give us a clue about this, for they represent divisions or groups of Roman citizens. The basic idea was that each assembly was made up of numerous blocks of citizens. Each century or tribe would vote internally first, thus arriving at a single vote for each group. For example, the tribal assembly was composed of 35 tribes: each tribe would arrive at a decision independently and then each tribe would constitute one vote in the assembly. The centuriate assembly worked in a similar way. There were 193 centuries of Roman citizens with each century arriving at a single vote before casting that single vote in the assembly. So in the tribal assembly, voting was always out of 35 and in the centuriate assembly out of 193. We now need to find out more detail about these 'centuries' and 'tribes'.

Exercise

Read the section in Beard and Crawford entitled 'Assemblies', Chapter Four, 'Political Institutions', pp.49–52. Concentrate initially on finding out what centuries and tribes were. Think about the following questions:

- What was the basis on which centuries were composed?
- What conclusions can we draw about how many citizens were in each century?
- What were 'tribes' and what factors determined into which tribes new citizens were enrolled?
- What might we infer about the number of citizens in each tribe?
- What other factors might have affected the way that tribes voted?

Discussion

Centuriate assembly
Centuries were timocratic: that is, they were composed according to

wealth. The property census, held every five years or so by the two censors, determined which century one belonged to. This harks back to the way the Roman army was organised and of course meant that the centuries of the élite, or the wealthy, had fewer members than those of the poorer citizens, yet their century's vote had equal weight in the assembly. We do not actually know how many citizens there were in each century, but we can make some important points. We do know that the *proletarii* were all in one single century and that there were eighteen centuries of equestrians at the other end of the spectrum. We also know that those in the first class, the group just below equestrians in terms of wealth, constituted 70 centuries. It is pretty obvious that there were many more poor citizens than wealthy, yet their individual votes were clearly far less significant. If the wealthiest two classes voted the same way, they could muster 88 votes in the assembly, very nearly a majority of the total of 193 centuries. It is also worth noting that voting took place in order of seniority; the wealthiest centuries voted first and as soon as a majority was achieved (i.e. 97 centuries voting the same way), the election was at an end. Therefore those in the lower centuries would hardly ever be called on to vote. The rich did not always vote as a cohesive single block, so the system was not quite as predictable as it first appears.

Figure 3.1   Reverse of a silver denarius, *c.*113–112 BCE, showing a Roman voting scene. The British Museum, London. © Copyright The Trustees of the British Museum. The voter on the left receives a voting tablet from an attendant at a lower level, while the voter on the right deposits his voting tablet in an urn.

Tribal assembly

Tribes were originally geographically or territorially based and by 241 BCE there were 31 rural or rustic tribes and four urban tribes. This number remained the same throughout the republican period, but many new citizens were created after this date. Italian 'allies' were given the citizenship en masse in the first century BCE and there were increasing numbers of freedmen being created. (Freedmen were slaves who had been freed and made Roman citizens, often on the death of their master or mistress.) There was a concerted attempt to enrol these new citizens into just a few tribes, regardless of where they lived. The apparent purpose of this was to limit their political influence in the tribal assembly. Once again, we don't know how many citizens there were in each tribe, but we do know that generally freedmen were always enrolled into one of the four urban tribes. So these urban tribes were composed primarily of the urban poor and freedmen. The élite, who had houses in Rome as well as in the countryside, would belong to one of the rural tribes, which had a much smaller membership. Of course, the vote of a rural tribe was worth as much in the tribal assembly as that of an urban tribe with a much greater number of citizens enrolled. So although tribes were not based on wealth in the same direct way as centuries, there was a clear policy of manipulating the system to ensure that there was always a majority of low-population rural tribes to which membership was strictly controlled. One might further suspect that the rural élite was far more likely to have had the time and means to vote in Rome, unlike poorer rural citizens. It is also thought that the relationship between wealthy landowners and their poorer neighbours would probably mean that a poor man could be relied on to vote in the same way as his local magnate.

I ought perhaps to mention here the concept of *clientela*. At its lowest level a poor citizen would be the client of a wealthy one, his patron. If he had a problem he might ask his patron for help – we know of patrons writing references, approving a potential husband for their client's daughter and helping with legal difficulties. His patron might also require some service of his client, it was common for high-ranking Romans to be followed about by a group of supporters and clients as they went about their daily business. The more clients a man had trailing after him, the more influential and powerful he would appear. The clients would be expected to support their patrons whenever they could, especially to further their political careers. It goes without saying that clients would be expected to vote for their patrons if they were standing for one of the magistracies. However, recently historians have begun to question whether the political importance of this relationship has been over-emphasised. There is further discussion of this subject in Section 1.2 of Block 4.

Conclusion

We have now looked in some detail at the three elements of the constitution and gained some understanding of how the system worked. I hope you have seen how we might challenge Polybius' view that 'one could reasonably argue ... that the constitution is a democracy' (6.14). But what about his notion of harmony and balance? How was this maintained when, to our modern eyes, the system looks so blatantly unfair? Well, if there was harmony or *concordia* when Polybius wrote his account, it soon began to evaporate. We can now move on to look at some important historical episodes which will help illustrate the stresses and strains which began to build up, and which ultimately tore the constitution apart. But before we do, let's turn back to an important question we posed earlier in this section and have not yet answered.

Exercise

Who made the laws in the republican system?

Discussion

The single word answer is 'magistrates'. The way the system was supposed to work is as follows: magistrates in consultation with the senate would devise legislation. Once the senate had agreed it, the proposed legislation would be put before the assembly, which could not amend it in any way, but simply vote for or against. However, recent research (Mouritsen, 2001) has come up with the interesting finding that the tribal assembly hardly ever voted against measures put before it. Only five cases of rejection by the assembly are documented between 167 and 104 BCE and none at all after that date. This perhaps suggests that bills were only presented to the assembly in the knowledge that they would be passed. It is known that laws had to be presented to the assembly several weeks before they were due to be voted on, at a non-decision-making meeting called a *contio*. Presumably bills which proved unpopular at this stage were either amended or withdrawn. So on this reading of the evidence it seems that the influence of the assembly on the actual shaping of legislation was greater than has been previously supposed.

2.3   The problems of imperial success

I mentioned at the beginning of this part that the acquisition of empire during the second century BCE had unforeseen consequences. In essence the problems which beset the later republican period and ultimately resulted in its breakdown were thought by many Romans to have been directly caused by their military successes. Sallust, writing in the 40s BCE, puts forward this thesis succinctly, as we shall see. Unlike both Appian and Polybius, Sallust was Roman. He was a member of the élite and embarked on the *cursus honorum*, reaching the tribunate in 52 BCE. Although he was expelled from the senate on charges of immoral and profligate living, he managed to reach the position of praetor by attaching himself to Julius Caesar, and ultimately he became governor of Africa Nova. When he enriched himself to such an extent in Africa that charges were preferred against him, Caesar intervened and Sallust withdrew from politics, now a very rich man, to write history until his death in 35 BCE. Ironically, given his somewhat murky past, there is a very strong moral dimension to Sallust's work and he uses history to make and illustrate moral points.

Exercise

Read Sallust's *The Conspiracy of Catiline* 1.10–13 in Reading 3.7. Think about the following questions:

- What particular aspects of foreign conquest were, according to Sallust, problematic?

- How did these problems manifest themselves?

- What does Sallust consider Rome's traditional virtues to have been?

Discussion

You were probably struck by Sallust's scathing critique of Rome. He seems to single out wealth, or love of money, as the greatest problem, but mentions increased leisure as well. You might also have picked up his implication towards the end of the passage that exposure to foreign luxury had corrupted those Roman soldiers who encountered it. In this instance he is specifically referring to Sulla's campaigns in the Greek east (87–84 BCE). The Greek east was the home of *luxuria*: according to Sallust and many others like him, *luxuria* was essentially a Greek disease against which Romans had little or no immunity. It is true that a huge increase in the number of slaves in this period would have meant more leisure for many. It is also true, as we have already seen, that more Romans became wealthier than ever before. You probably also gained a strong sense that there had once been a 'golden age', a time when men were ambitious only for virtue and honour. Along with honesty, piety and modesty, these were old-fashioned virtues and values being rapidly eroded in a new world order where Rome was becoming the only superpower. This notion of a 'golden age' is a common theme throughout Latin literature – and perhaps as universal today as in the days of Sallust.

Cato the Elder

One man who throughout Roman history was thought to have embodied traditional Roman virtues was Marcus Porcius Cato, or Cato the Elder, sometimes know as Cato the Censor. He lived between 234 and 149 BCE and has left us the earliest surviving prose work in the Latin language: *De Agri Cultura* (*On Agriculture*), written about 160 BCE. It is a practical and contemporary manual on farming derived from the writer's personal experience. However, as you will see, Cato was far from being just a farmer.

Exercise

Read the entry for Cato the Elder in the *OCCC*. Jot down some brief biographical points, including his career path (dates of his magistracies, military service, etc.). As you do so, look back at the work you did on the *cursus honorum*. How well does Cato's career fit the pattern?

Discussion

You probably noted that Cato was a *novus homo*, or 'new man', and that he fought in the Second Punic War against Hannibal. I've also picked out the following. He was a quaestor in 204, again on military service. He was aedile in 199 and praetor in 198. He then went on to govern Sardinia and attained the consulship in 195. After that he served as a governor in Spain for which he was awarded a triumph. He was elected censor in 184 by promising to reverse the decline of traditional morality. You may also have noted that throughout his life he was busy as an advocate (and sometimes a defendant) in the courts, which implies that he was an effective orator and skilled in rhetoric. Of course, this account is modern scholarship and relies for its information on ancient sources. The two most important ancient sources for Cato's life are his own *De Agri Cultura* and the biography of him written later by Plutarch.

Plutarch was Greek, like many of the ancient writers you have encountered so far. He was born in the mid 40s of the first century CE and died around 120. His most famous work is *Parallel Lives*: a series of short biographies of famous Greeks and Romans. A Greek 'life' was paired with a Roman 'life' and they were designed to complement one another. This arrangement was probably designed to show both Greeks and Romans that each had great men and a history worth celebrating.

Exercise

Now read the excerpts from Cato's *De Agri Cultura* and Plutarch's *Life of Cato the Elder* in Readings 3.8 and 3.9. Think about the strengths and weaknesses of each account. How far do you consider the accounts to be useful or reliable as historical sources? Which source would you choose if you were writing a biography of Cato? (Don't get too bogged down in the detail at this point: just get a general impression of each source.)

Discussion

Cato: De Agri Cultura

An obvious strength of this source is that it is contemporary. It is also written by Cato himself, so it might give us some insight into his character. The book appears to be a practical handbook, and we might therefore assume that it was meant to be read by those about to acquire a country estate but who were not experienced farmers. This *could* indicate its reliability as a source, in the sense that it was probably not written with a hidden agenda. We do however need to be cautious. A weakness might be that because it is written by Cato himself, it is bound to portray him in a favourable light. Its didacticism also means that it is quite narrowly focused, so does not tell us a lot of things about Cato that we would like to know.

Plutarch: Life of Cato

The obvious weakness with this source is that it is not contemporary: in fact it was written about two and half centuries after Cato the Elder died. However, you probably felt that it tells us a great deal more about Cato's character. It certainly does present a more rounded picture of the man, more critical but nevertheless praising Cato's perceived virtues. As mentioned earlier, Plutarch wrote his short biographies or *Lives* in pairs, with a Greek and a Roman considered together. So even if you read the entire 'Life' of Cato the Elder it would still be out of context unless you read it alongside the life of Aristides, the fifth-century Athenian general with whom Cato was paired. This is because the two biographies were designed to complement and illuminate one another. A further weakness of this source might be the purpose for which it was written: to entertain an élite, primarily male audience. Plutarch therefore may have sought to spice up his account a little to make it more interesting. For example, Plutarch's assertion that 'the men (male slaves) could sleep with the women slaves of the establishment, for a fixed price' (21). It is rather neat because it confirms one of Plutarch's themes – Cato's parsimoniousness – but there is also the sexual aspect of the arrangement where we are presented with Cato as *leno* or pimp.

Let's move now to content. What do these sources tell us that is historically useful?

Exercise

Read the Cato passage again (Reading 3.8) and think how we might use it to support a historical point that connects in some way with the work we have already done in this part. For example, can you find any evidence which we might use in a discussion of the land problem?

Discussion

This is a bit more tricky but I'm hoping you thought that the Cato extract is good evidence for the idea that, during the second century BCE, many large agricultural estates were increasingly being worked by slave labourers. As we have seen, the slaves were a result of Rome's successful wars, so this was a relatively new phenomenon and one that was to have important political consequences. This source could be used as evidence for an increase in the number of men who were acquiring rural estates, thus creating a demand for a practical handbook of this type. There is also the suggestion that the new owner would only visit the estate periodically. So in this passage we have evidence for large estates, worked by slave labour, owned by absentee landlords with little farming experience. We might also infer that this was a relatively new and increasingly common phenomenon.

Exercise

Now read the Plutarch extract again (Reading 3.9). What points might you pull out of this extract which we could use to comment on the work we have already done in this part? How, for example, might it be used to advance a discussion of morality and *luxuria*?

Discussion

In many ways this is a much richer source. You probably noted Plutarch's emphasis on Cato's 'old fashioned' virtues. He lived a comparatively simple and frugal life for a man of his class. Cato appears to have been proud of building and maintaining this image and we can perhaps infer that there was a political dimension to this. Plutarch suggests that he may have created this image in order to show his contemporaries the correct way to behave 'so as to correct and restrain the extravagance of others'(*Life of Cato* 5). It is interesting that there is no hint in Plutarch's account of Cato behaving hypocritically. The criticism that is levelled mainly focuses on Cato's lack of humanity, especially towards slaves. You can see how a good link can be made in this respect between the two ancient sources we are considering. Cato was clearly famous for the way in which he treated his slaves.

You probably also noticed Plutarch's inclusion of Cato's tirade against the Greeks and their culture. This is quite interesting for several reasons. First, Plutarch was Greek. During Cato's life Rome had only recently conquered Greece and the Greek east and many Greek slaves found their way to Rome. Some of these slaves, however, were well educated and often became secretaries, doctors, teachers and so on. One can imagine how this issue might have had particular resonance with Plutarch, writing several centuries later. There is a certain irony here and I think a whiff of hypocrisy, for Cato didn't just write his handbook on farming; he also wrote a history of Rome (of which only fragments survive) and was a noted orator. His literary and rhetorical skills owed a huge debt to Greek culture. He must have consciously studied Greek literature and oratory in order to adapt it for a Roman audience. At the very beginning of the extract Plutarch tells us that Cato became known as the 'Roman Demosthenes' (Demosthenes was a famous Athenian orator of the fourth century BCE). Rome's cultural debt to Greece was huge: in Latin literature, art, architecture and philosophy, the influence of Greece is clear. Even Rome's origins had been tied into the cycle of Greek myth through the story of Aeneas, the Trojan prince who escaped the destruction of Troy and went on to establish the Roman people in Italy. Yet despite all this, the relationship between Romans and Greeks was always a little uneasy and ambiguous.

Exercise

Look at the two sources again (Readings 3.8 and 3.9). This time try to find direct links between the two sources. Are there points within the two sources which confirm one another?

Discussion

You probably managed to find areas where our two sources support one another. Both feature slaves quite heavily and both state that Cato felt it sensible to sell slaves when they became too old or too ill to be productive. 'Sell worn out oxen … an old slave, a sickly slave' he advises in *De Agri Cultura* 2. Plutarch writes that 'when they became too old to work, he felt it his duty to sell them' (*Life of Cato* 4). Both sources also make the point that slaves should be kept busy the whole time. In fact, taken together, these sources would seem to provide a good insight into how Cato felt that slaves should be treated.

The two sources also corroborate each other in a broader and more general way. I would suggest that one can see Plutarch's Cato in the manual on farming. His frugality, his parsimony, his conservatism and rather strict morality, are all apparent in these sources. But of course we do need to be cautious. Plutarch is not a contemporary source. We might assume that he used Cato's own writings when he composed his life of Cato, so in this sense Plutarch would technically be an ancient secondary source. Therefore it shouldn't surprise us too much if there is a degree of agreement between the two sources. Cato became an iconic figure after his death in 149 BCE, and he remained a figurehead for those Romans who championed traditional, conservative values throughout the remainder of the republican period and beyond. Because of this a 'tradition' about him would have been well established by Plutarch's time, which to some extent he must be reflecting.

References

Ancient sources

Polybius, *The Rise of the Roman Empire* 1.1, in I. Scott-Kilvert (trans.) (1979) *Polybius: The Rise of the Roman Empire*, London: Penguin.

Thucydides, *The History of the Peloponnesian War*, in R. Crawley (trans.) (1997) *Thucydides: The History of the Peloponnesian War*, Ware: Wordsworth.

Modern scholarship

Mouritsen, H. (2001) *Plebs and Politics in the Late Roman Republic*, Cambridge and New York, Cambridge University Press.

Further reading

Modern scholarship

Crawford, M. (1992) *The Roman Republic* (2nd edn), London: Fontana.

Part 3 Building history: ancestors, achievements and children

3.1 Introduction

It will be abundantly clear to you by now that society in Rome was very structured and hierarchical. As you have seen, the status of individuals was defined in a wide variety of ways: by their political status, age, wealth, rank or morality. Achieving these different forms of status contributed to establishing a reputation. Cato, for example, gained a reputation and was particularly remembered for his traditional values. A successful political career always brought high status, but there were other, more glamorous, ways of achieving a reputation. An honourable reputation brought glory and respect to a family, so that maintaining the reputation (and its associated status) became an imperative of descendants and relations. To begin with, we will investigate some ways of achieving fame and reputation.

As you have learned, high political rank such as the consulship was not passed from hand to hand by members of the elite, and could not actually be inherited from father to son. Rank, in the republic at least, had to be achieved rather than simply ascribed to an individual. It is worth considering the pressure on a young élite male to succeed. Despite the undoubted advantages of belonging to one of the great families, there were also great expectations. Young men were expected to match the exploits and successes of their ancestors and if possible exceed them. You will be going on to study some of these family exploits by studying historical examples. But before then we should consider how the positive values that constituted a good reputation were presented in Roman literature, and how role-models may have contributed to the aspirations of young (or old) Romans.

You have already come across some related examples of 'good reputation' in the course: Homer's heroes (Block 1), the Athenian dead (Block 2), and in the previous part of this block, episodes from the life of Cato were held up as examples. Latin used the same word, *exemplum* (plural: *exempla*) to describe episodes from history or biography that were used to illustrate the correct or righteous behaviour (and sometimes the opposite) of individuals. *Exempla* are a striking element of the genre of Roman history and Livy, the most famous Roman historian, provides many examples of this literary device (Chaplin, 2000). However, Livy's *exempla* appear as a part of his continuous narrative of the history of Rome and the models of behaviour and object-lessons are woven seamlessly into the story. They appear either as inspiring episodes narrating the history that serve as examples in their own right, or they occur within the narrative as past events referred back to and providing an example relevant to the current circumstance. This doesn't mean that Livy's history is simply a moral tale and not a useful history, but is does mean that when reading Livy it is necessary to be aware that a story is being told, and to note how and why it is told. This is true whether Livy is recounting legendary events in the distant past, which may have some element of historical fact within them, or events closer to his own lifetime.

Exercise

First let's look at a set of episodes from the legendary early history of the Roman republic (Livy 2.10–13 in Reading 3.10). The last Etruscan king of Rome, Tarquinius Superbus, has been deposed, but tries to return to power with the aid of Lars Porsenna, the Etruscan King of Clusium (modern Chiusi): the republic fights back. As you read, identify the four *exempla* (one in each chapter) and note down the leading protagonist in each *exemplum*. Also note the virtues they embody.

Discussion

1   The first *exemplum* is the famous story of how Horatius held the bridge (see Figures 3.2 and 3.3). His manifest virtues include heroism, loyalty, and bravery (at the very least). Notice Livy saying that the story is more celebrated than believed, making it indirectly apparent that it exists for its inspirational qualities rather than factual ones.

2   The second *exemplum* is less dramatic, but the cunning plan of Valerius provides an example of brains defeating brawn.

3   The third, more shocking *exemplum*, sees Mucius failing in his brave assassination attempt, but then providing a remarkable example of Roman courage, resolve and fortitude by burning off his own hand.

4   Finally Cloelia, inspired by Mucius, shows that not only the men of Rome are formidable, by a display of courage and modest wisdom, and is rewarded with an equestrian statue.

There is more that could be drawn from these famous episodes, but a recurrent theme is how the bravery and resourcefulness of the Roman heroes impresses the enemy king who ends up respecting them as a result of their actions. The *exempla* therefore demonstrate the rewards

Figures 3.2 and 3.3 Bronze medallion of the emperor Antoninus Pius minted between CE 140–144, depicting the feat of Horatius Cocles. Bibliothèque nationale de France.

of virtuous behaviour in the context of military and political conflict. *Exempla* such as these were not confined to literary history. A poem by Martial (*c.*CE 40–102) celebrates the bravery of Mucius, describing a re-enactment of the scene in the amphitheatre where a criminal had to enact the role of Mucius Scaevola as a punishment:

> The spectacle which is now presented to us on Caesar's arena, was the great glory of the days of Brutus. See how bravely the hand bears the flames. It even enjoys the punishment, and reigns in the astonished fire! Scaevola himself appears as a spectator of his own act, and applauds the noble destruction of his right hand, which seems to luxuriate in the sacrificial fire; and unless the means of suffering had been taken away from it against its will, the left hand was still more boldly preparing to meet the vanquished flames. I am unwilling, after so glorious an action, to inquire what he had done before; it is sufficient for me to have witnessed the fate of his hand.
>
> (Martial, *Epigrams* 8.30)

The second account is more subtle, and it precedes a number of brave individual actions in Livy's narrative. It is an episode from the Second Punic War – a time closer to Livy – and in the realms of reliable history rather than myth. It is part of the (heroic) story of how Scipio Africanus, as he became known, defeated Rome's most serious enemy, Hannibal the Carthaginian. The conflict was long, with many glorious and inglorious episodes and you will be reading only a very small part of the story here. In 209 BCE Rome was fighting back after a series of defeats and Scipio was leading his troops fighting against the Carthaginians in Spain. (You will find more information in the *OCCC* under 'Rome (history)', 'Scipio Africanus' and 'Hannibal'.)

Exercise

Read the passage from Livy 26.41 (Reading 3.11) and, as before, identify the principal *exemplum* and any minor examples you read.

Rather than simply describing a heroic exploit, this extract is a more general lesson from the past, an example of Roman rhetoric put into the mouth of Scipio by Livy. Therefore I'd like you to think about the overall message delivered and note down the main themes of the speech.

Discussion

> Within Scipio's exhortation to the troops is the broad *exemplum* that
> defeat often precedes a victory. At a more detailed level various
> aspects of the speech may be identified as *exempla* – references to
> earlier events (or stories) that provide instruction for the present. In his
> speech to the troops, Scipio highly praises their previous conduct –
> they are an example to themselves. He also strongly emphasises the
> role of his father and uncle who were both recently killed in the
> conflict in Spain. Their past achievement (until defeated), as well as
> the track record of his family, serve as an example of what the troops
> (and Rome) can expect from their general. Specific examples of past
> heroics are referred to: for example, the reference to Porsenna.
> However the central part of the speech is a résumé of the war with
> Hannibal. (Note that Scipio excuses himself from the most serious
> military disasters for Rome at Trebia, Lake Trasimene and Cannae.)
> These form the necessary prelude to the Roman victory. In the final
> section he extrapolates from the past – with divine aid, but also with
> the aid of his own intellect – the Roman victory. He is predicting the
> future with the lessons of the past. The speech ends by returning to
> where it began: with his father and uncle he will live up to their
> example with his courage ability and honour; it will be as if they are
> reborn. Livy is writing with the benefit of hindsight nearly 200 years
> after the events and so he can guarantee the accuracy of the
> predictions and how the lesson to be taken from the past came to be
> fulfilled.

Even if Livy can be considered an ancient secondary source, and a skilful
writer of rhetoric and history, the desire expressed by Scipio to live up to
the achievements of his ancestors was a potent force in Roman élite families
and it may be traced back directly to the time of Scipio.

3.2   The tomb of the Scipios

Just off the Via Appia, outside the walls of republican Rome, lies the tomb
of the Scipios. It dates to the third and second centuries BCEand houses the
remains of six generations of the Cornelii Scipiones. The most famous
member of the family – Publius Cornelius Scipio Africanus, the man who
defeated Hannibal – was not buried here, but many of his relations were,
including his paternal grandfather and great-grandfather who built the
tomb. It is a subterranean rock-cut tomb, quite unusual in a Roman context
and closely resembling Etruscan rock-cut tombs. It had a façade structured
with columns and ornamented with statues and traces of wall paintings

which appear to have depicted exploits of the family (Figure 3.4). A series of passages and chambers excavated into the soft tufo rock form a square in plan with a cross in the centre. The interconnecting passages are the setting for the sarcophagi that contained the remains of the Scipios (Figure 3.5). This is an unusual feature of the tomb: cremation was the usual practice rather than inhumation in stone sarcophagi. Upon these sarcophagi were inscribed *elogia* to the deceased, and these inscriptions clearly record the aspirations and achievements of one of the leading republican families of Rome.

In the following exercises you will work through the surviving epitaphs in the order of the deaths of the individuals buried in the tomb. The text of the inscriptions has been translated for you to read and study, but original Latin is also provided to give you a sense of the original language. If you have already studied some Latin you will find some of the word forms unfamiliar. The Latin that is usually taught is that which was used between *c*.90 BCE and *c*.CE 120, but the Latin inscribed on these tombs dates back to nearly two hundred years earlier, when written Latin was only just beginning to develop into what we now know as Classical Latin.

At the end of the main corridor, and facing the entrance, is the sarcophagus of Lucius Cornelius Scipio Barbatus (the founder of the tomb) who died in about 280 BCE. The elaborate sarcophagus is shaped like an altar and decorated with architectural motifs (Figure 3.6). His name, 'Lucius Cornelius Scipio Barbatus, son of Gnaius', is inscribed on the edge of the lid. Some time later his *elogium* was inscribed on the sarcophagus itself; at a later time still the first line and a half were erased: what they said and why they were erased is not known.

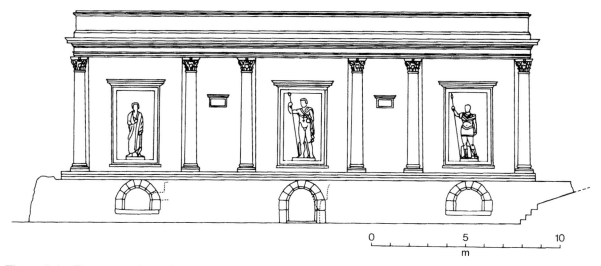

Figure 3.4   Reconstruction of the façade of the tomb of the Scipios, from Filippo Coarelli and Luisanna Usai, *Guida Archeologica di Roma*, Arnoldo Mondadori Editore, 1974, p.327.

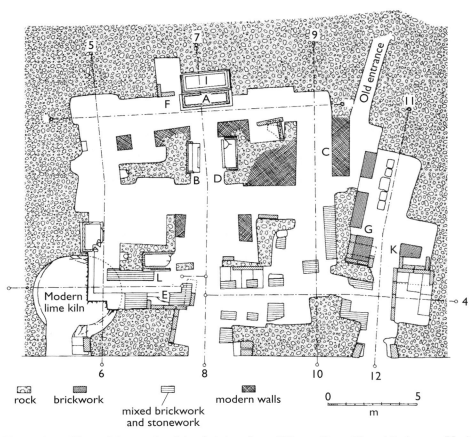

Figure 3.5   Plan of the tomb of the Scipios, from Filippo Coarelli and Luisanna Usai, *Guida Archeologica di Roma*, Arnoldo Mondadori Editore, 1974, p.326. The letters indicate the find spots of the sarcophagi or epitaphs (see Plate 39 in the Illustrations Book for the Scipio family tree).

A brief digression on inscriptions

The texts of thousands of Roman inscriptions in Latin that have been found are collected in a vast set of printed volumes called the *Corpus Inscriptionum Latinarum*, abbreviated to *CIL*. Latin inscriptions are identified and referred to by their entry in this catalogue. So the next inscription you will study is referred to as *CIL* VI 1284. This means the text of the inscription can be found as entry 1284 in volume six of the *Corpus Inscriptionum Latinarum*. (Page numbers are not used as giving the catalogue entry number is enough.) The volumes are only to be found in specialist libraries, but some of them have been made available on the internet. On the course website you will find links to more information about the *CIL*. Compilation started in the nineteenth century in Germany and so much of the information about the catalogue is in German, and the text of the volumes is almost entirely

Figure 3.6 Sarcophagus of L. Cornelius Scipio Barbatus. Vatican Archive XVIII-19-12. Photo: Vatican Museums.

written in Latin. A useful description of the *CIL* is to be found in the first chapter of Bodel (2001).

Exercise

Read the *elogium* of Lucius Cornelius Scipio Barbatus below. It is written in the Saturnine metre, an early form of Latin verse. The first line identifies him. Pick out the achievements noted in the remaining three lines. (All the translations are my own.)

> Cornelius Lucius Scipio Barbatus Gnaivod patre
> prognatus fortis vir sapiensque quoius forma virtutei parisuma
> fuit consol censor aidilis quei fuit apud vos Taurasia Cisauna
> Samnio cepit subigit omne Loucanam opsidesque abd oucit
> *CIL* VI 1284

Translation

> Lucius Cornelius Scipio Barbatus, descended from his father Gnaius.
> A strong and wise man whose appearance was equal to his valour.
> He was Consul, Censor, Aedile amongst you. Taurasia and Cisauna
> in Samnium he captured, he subjugated all of Lucania and carried away hostages.

Discussion

On the second line his physical and mental virtues are noted; on the third, the high political ranks he achieved in his civil career, leading into the fourth line citing his military achievements. The use of the second person 'you' suggests that the inscription records a public eulogy that was read at the funeral.

Exercise

Now read his son Lucius Cornelius Scipio's epitaph below. Pick out his qualities and achievements and compare them to those of his father. (The epitaph on the sarcophagus was incised later in the early second century and replaces one and a half lines with Saturnine verse.)

On the lid

> L Cornelio L f Scipio
> aidiles cosol cesor
> *CIL* VI 1286

Translation

Lucius Cornelius Scipio son of Lucius
Aedile, Consul and Censor.

On the sarcophagus

L(ucius) Cornelio(s) L(uci) f(ililus) Scipio
aidiles cosol cesor honc oino ploirume cosentiont R[omane]
duonoro optumo fuise viro
Luciom Scipione filios Barbati
consol censor aidilis hic fuet a[pud vos]
hec cepit Corsica Aleriaque urbe
dedet Tempestatebus aide mereto[d]
CIL VI 1287

Translation

Lucius Cornelius Scipio son of Lucius.
Aedile, Consul and Censor.
The majority of Romans agree that this man alone was the best
of the aristocrats.
This man, Lucius Scipio, son of Barbatus, was Consul, Censor
and Aedile amongst you.
This man captured Corsica and the city of Aleria.
He dedicated a temple to the storm god for favours received.

Discussion

Here the epitaph is similar to his father's: the political and military
achievements are highlighted, but the personal qualities are
generalised. His being 'the best' and his descent are both emphasised
by the naming of his father on the sarcophagus.

Exercise

Read the next three epitaphs of members of the following generations.
(Plate 39 in your Illustrations Book shows the family tree identifying
those commemorated in the tomb.) Note down how they differ from
the preceding two.

Publius Cornelius, son of Publius c.180 BCE, and grandson of Scipio Africanus

Quei apice insigne Dial[is fl]aminis gesistei
mors perfec[it] tua ut essent omnia
brevia honos fama virtusque
gloria atque ingenium quibus sei
in longa licuiset tibe utier vita
facile facteis superases gloriam

maiorum qua re lubens te in gremiu
Scipio recipit terra Publi
prognatum Publio Corneli
CIL VI 1288

Translation

You who wore the conical cap, the insignia of the High Priest of
Jupiter.
Death made all short-lived your honour, fame, courage,
Glory and genius. If you could have enjoyed a longer life,
You would easily have surpassed by your deeds the glory of your
Ancestors. For this, the earth willingly receives you into her
bosom
Publius Cornelius Scipio, descendant of Publius.

Lucius Cornelius Scipio, son of Gnaius

L(ucius) Cornelius Cn(aei) f(ilius) Cn(aei) n(epos) Scipio
magna sapientia
multasque virtutes aetate quom parva
posidet hoc saxsum quoiei vita defecit non
hono honore is hic situs quei nunquam
victus est virtutei annos gnatus XX is
l[oc]eis mandatus ne quairatis honore
quei minus sit mandatus
CIL VI 1289

Translation

Lucius Cornelius Scipio, son of Gnaius, grandson of Gnaius,
A great wisdom,
Much courage, but little age,
Is contained in this rock.
To achieve honours he lacked life, not honour, he who lies here.
He was never beaten in courage. At the age of twenty,
He was entrusted to this place, do not ask about his honours,
He was entrusted with none.

Lucius Cornelius Scipio, son of Lucius, quaestor in 167 BCE

L(ucius) Cornelius L(uci) f(ilius) P(ubli) n(epos)
Scipio quaist(or)
tr(ibunus) mil(itum) annos
gnatus XXXIII
mortuos pater
regem Antioco(m)
subegit
CIL VI 1290

Translation

Lucius Cornelius Scipio, son of Lucius, grandson of Publius.
Quaestor,
Military Tribune.
Died aged thirty-three.
His father defeated king Antiochus.

Discussion

These three Cornelii all died young. Some achieved some minor political, military or religious rank. There is some mention of their personal qualities. The key thing I noted is that in place of high achievements we see an emphasis on their descent and forebears: fathers and grandfathers are named, sometimes with their achievements. Failure to achieve high status is explained and excused by a premature death.

Exercise

In contrast to young sons, the women of the family – who did not have political or military careers – are commemorated differently. Read the epitaph of Paulla, probably the mother of the Lucius Cornelius, son of Gnaius, commemorated in *CIL* VI 1289 above. What were her achievements?

[P]aulla Cornelia Cn(aei) f(ilia) Hispalli
CIL VI 1294

Translation

Paulla Cornelia, daughter of Gnaius, wife of Hispallus.

Discussion

She is only commemorated with reference to her father and husband. Her achievement is her place within the dynasty – defined only with reference to the males. Her fundamental role of raising the next generation of Cornelii is not commemorated despite its importance.

Exercise

The epitaph of (probably) her other son Gnaeus Cornelius Scipio, who was praetor in 139 BCE and who probably died around 130 BCE, encapsulates the difference in the ways that males and females were commemorated and also the importance of maintaining the honour of the family in the constant competition with one's ancestors.

Read the following inscription and jot down notes about its structure. Think about how it emphasises the themes of family and ancestry.

Gnaeus Cornelius Scipio Hispanus, son of Gnaius

Cn(aeus) Cornelius Cn(aei) f(ilius) Scipio Hispanus
pr(aetor) aid(ilis) cur(ulis) q(uaestor) tr(ibunus) mil(itum) II Xvir sl(itibus) iudik(andis)
Xvir sacr(is) fac(iundis)
virtutes generis mieis moribus accumulavi
progeniem genui facta patris petiei
maiorum optenui laudem ut sibei me esse creatum
laetentur stirpem nobilitavit honor

CIL VI 1293

Translation

Gnaius Cornelius Scipio Hispanus, son of Gnaius,
Praetor, Curule Aedile, Quaestor, Military Tribune twice,
Magistrate in legal affairs,
Magistrate in religious affairs,
I have enhanced by my habits the accumulated virtues of my forebears,
I produced sons and equalled the deeds of my father.
I have obtained the praise of my ancestors who were proud to have created me.
My honours have ennobled the lineage.

Discussion

The inscription is in two parts. It begins by listing the deceased's official achievements: civil, military and religious. You can see how far he climbed the *cursus honorum*. He reached the second highest office of praetor but did not attain the consulship. In the second part his family and ancestors take over. He had children, which was important as it meant the family would continue, although obviously without the need to record the contribution of his wife! The epitaph also mentions Gnaeus' own father, and it was clearly important to try to live up to his reputation. Gnaeus' life is then put in the context of his family line (the *gens*) as a whole. Note how his ancestors are treated as if they are aware of the achievements of their descendants. There is a strong sense that all of your ancestors are looking over your shoulder. This is perhaps emphasised by the use of the first person, copying Greek models that later became standard in aristocratic *elogia*.

The tomb of the Scipios provides a uniquely detailed insight into the deeds and aspirations of the Cornelii, which closely matches sentiments put into the mouth of Scipio by Livy. But there is a range of further evidence that establishes how important ancestors were.

3.3 Public commemoration

Exercise

Read Polybius 6.53 in Reading 3.12 and note down the ways in which ancestors and the family generally were celebrated. Look as well at the image of a Roman man carrying two portrait busts of his ancestors in Plate 40 of the Illustrations Book.

Discussion

In this passage Polybius is primarily concerned with the funerals of the élite. He describes how they would become a public event in the forum. He also mentions how funerary speeches given by a close male relative (ideally a son) of the deceased were an important feature of élite funerals. Polybius seems to imply that only dead *men* received such treatment, but we do know of noble women who were given a similar send-off. Polybius then describes how a portrait of the dead man was placed in the family home. He seems to be describing some sort of mask, which could be 'worn' by the dead man, and tells us that part of the funeral ritual involved members of the family wearing the masks of their illustrious ancestors; they also dressed appropriately according to the rank achieved by the ancestor concerned. So, for a family like the Scipios, who could boast 30 consuls in 200 years or so, this aspect of the funeral would have been extremely impressive. It would have linked the dead man into a chain of achievement stretching back through the generations. There would also be a link to future generations by the dead man's son or other close and youthful male relative who would deliver the funeral speech.

Polybius ends by saying that some Romans put their country before themselves, and then goes on in 6.55 to provide an example. The *exemplum* he uses is the story of Horatius Cocles as a model of enthusiasm for noble deeds and for emulation.

Exercise

These funeral speeches were sometimes recorded for posterity and Pliny the Elder, who wrote in the first century CE (he was killed during the eruption of Vesuvius in 79), quotes from a funeral speech given in the third century BCE, showing us that the speech had been preserved. The funeral was for L.Caecilius Metellus who died in 221 BCE. His son, who reached the consulship in 205, spoke the funeral oration.

Read an extract from the speech below. What do you notice about the language of the speech? What does it tell us about competitiveness and ambition?

> L.Metellus was a *pontifex*, twice consul, dictator, master of horse, and *quindecimvir* for the distribution of land; he was the first to lead elephants in a triumphal procession, during the first Punic war. In the funeral oration, his son Q.Metellus wrote:
>
> 'He achieved the ten greatest and best things, which wise men spend their whole lives seeking. He wished to be the first of warriors, the best of orators, and the most valiant of commanders; to be in charge of the greatest affairs and held in the greatest honour; to possess supreme wisdom and be regarded as supreme in the senate; to come to great wealth by honourable means; to leave many children; and to be the most distinguished person in the state. These things he achieved, and none but he achieved them since Rome was founded.'
>
> (Pliny the Elder, *Natural Histories* 7.139–40)

Discussion

What strikes me initially about this passage is its use of superlatives: first, best, greatest (*primus*, *optimus*, *maximus*). It gives a wonderful sense of what was considered important to élite Roman males. We have already noted that in order to reach the top one had to be a soldier and a politician, and this excerpt makes that clear. We have warrior and commander juxtaposed with orator and 'supreme in the senate'. There is also the link to family: 'leave many children' and wealth, although honourable means are stressed. So generally élite men aspired to being *primus inter pares* or 'first among equals'. Which brings us back to the point about how competitive this system was and how dangerous and potentially destructive it could be.

Does this *elogium* remind you in any way of Pericles' Funeral Speech in Thucydides, which you studied in Block 2?

Élite Italians: burial traditions

So far in this part of the block we have been studying the attitudes and burials of the élite in Rome. It is also possible to investigate the burials of high-status individuals in other parts of Italy, even if we do not have the literary evidence to go along with the archaeology.

You have already met at Poseidonia one example of a strongly developed representation of the status of the deceased (you may wish to review DVD3, Section 1, which you watched in Section 1.3 of this block). Here the Lucanian élite emphasised the status of males by representing them in their full war panoply in the painted tombs; furthermore, they were often buried in their ceremonial armour within the tombs. Women too were represented in death by being dressed in their finery, which acted as if to transfer their status in life to the underworld.

The wall paintings are spectacular, but how far are the images simply conventional representations of the men and women? The relative rarity of the painted tombs in the cemeteries of Poseidonia suggests that the tombs belonged to the élite, and this is supported by the finds of feasting equipment in the tombs. Yet there is no attempt at individual characterisation. The image is of a warrior only, and not of a recognisable individual: it represents the status, not the person. In the tomb of the Scipios the situation was different: individuals were not visually represented on the sarcophagi (although they may have been on the walls of the exterior of the tomb) but their deeds and achievements *were* recorded in the inscriptions. The epitaphs convey a set of conventional representations of the *cursus honorum*, yet they convey little personal information beyond idealised qualities such as courage and genius. As you saw, these qualities are only ascribed to the men: we are told nothing of female qualities. Outside Rome, in Etruria to the north, women were accorded a higher status and this was reflected in their tombs. For example, in painted tombs they are shown participating at banquets, unlike in Poseidonia.

A spectacular find from Chiusi (in modern Tuscany) of the terracotta sarcophagus of an Etruscan noble woman, Seianti Hanunia Tlesnasa, provides a unique opportunity to investigate the life of an élite woman and consider how she was commemorated after death. (The sarcophagus, now in the British Museum, still contains her bones.) She lived between about 250 and 150 BCE and was probably born after the foundation of the Roman colony of Paestum around the time of the First Punic War. She may have died while Hannibal was ravaging southern Italy during the Second Punic War and her burial most likely took place around 200 BCE.

Exercise

Now watch DVD3, Section 2 on Seianti Hanunia Tlesnasa. As you watch, note down the sources of evidence and techniques used in the investigation of the sarcophagus and the skeleton. How do the sources and methodologies influence what can be reconstructed of Seianti's life?

Discussion

Clearly the investigation of the skeleton and the facial reconstruction provide a whole new area of knowledge about the deceased. We simply do not have the same quality of evidence for the Scipios or the Lucanians of Poseidonia. This means that it is possible to say far more about Seianti as an individual, and the traumatic events in her life, than we can about the others. All we know about the deceased Scipios and the deceased Lucanians is how they were commemorated. What is more, in the case of Seianti, it is also possible to combine evidence of funeral rituals – how she was commemorated and represented in her monument with the physical evidence for her appearance and fitness. This means that it is possible to go beyond interpreting her sarcophagus as only representing her élite status: it can also be interpreted as individually representing her physical form, at least to some extent.

The osteological investigation revealed unsuspected aspects of ritual treatment of the corpse, a reminder that the evidence from burials is the result of ritual practice, and that conventionalised representations of the dead (i.e. the figure on the sarcophagus) also had a role in funerary rituals. Applying new and different approaches to the study of the sarcophagus creates and enhances understanding of both the evidence itself – the sarcophagus and burial – and also the actual individual who lived in the past.

3.4   Genealogies

By now you will have become aware of the role of commemoration and the necessity of living up to the achievements of ancestors in Roman élite society. In the remainder of this part you will first discover how Roman personal names were used and what they signified – this will help you keep track of dynasties such as the Cornelii Scipiones. (This section is intended for reference purposes only: you are not expected to memorise it.) Then you will study some of the roles that genealogies performed in the society of the living in Rome: these roles will be related to further elements of competition in Roman culture.

Roman names: a survival guide

A Roman citizen's name was known as a *trianomina*, because it had three parts (*tria* = three; *nomina* = names). These parts are called the *praenomen*, the *nomen* and the *cognomen*. So Gaius Iulius Caesar had the *praenomen* Gaius, the *nomen* Iulius and the *cognomen* Caesar.

The *praenomen* can be thought of like an English first name or given name. These were selected from a limited range and sometimes made reference to the circumstances of a birth. For example: Lucius = 'born by day'; Manius = 'born in the morning'; Quintus = 'the fifth'; Decimus = 'the tenth'. Over time, however, they gradually lost all connection with their meaning. As a rule the eldest son was given the same *praenomen* as his father. The *praenomen* is usually abbreviated in inscriptions and writing. These are the abbreviations of the most common names:

A.	Aulus
Ap(p).	Appius
C.	Gaius
Cn.	Gnaeus
D.	Decimus
L.	Lucius
M.	Marcus
M'.	Manius
N.	Numerius
P.	Publius
Q.	Quintus
Ser.	Servius
Sex. (or S.)	Sextus
Sp.	Spurius
T.	Titus
Ti.	Tiberius

Roman citizens were divided into groups called a *gens* (plural *gentes*). In theory all members of a *gens* shared a common ancestor. All members of a *gens* also shared a common name – the *nomen*. So Gaius Iulius Caesar, with the *nomen* Iulius, was a member of the *gens* Iulia. Because *gens* is a feminine noun in Latin, *gentes* are referred to in their feminine form, even though all traditional Roman *nomina* (plural of *nomen*) ended in '-ius', the masculine ending. Very often whole *gentes* are referred to by using the plural of their shared *nomen*, so the Iulii are all the members of the *gens* Iulia, sharing the *nomen* (if they are men) Iulius.

To this was added the *cognomen*, a family name shared by members of the same family. So Gaius Iulius Caesar belonged to the Caesar family of the *gens* Iulia. If a family became very large, a second family name might be added to distinguish individuals who would otherwise have the same names: for example, Lucius Cornelius Lentulus Crus and Lucius Cornelius Lentulus Niger. The *cognomen* was often derived from a personal characteristic: in this case Crus = 'leg' and Niger = 'swarthy'. In some complicated cases a third *cognomen* could also be added.

Sometimes a final part of a name might be added to an individual to commemorate some great achievement (and was used as a sort of nickname). For example, Publius Cornelius Scipio Africanus was given the name 'Africanus', meaning African, after defeating Hannibal. Such a name was usually only applied to an individual and did not pass on to descendants. (It is sometimes called an *agnomen*, although this isn't an ancient term.)

Another factor which might have further complicated a name is if an individual was adopted from one *gens* to another. This is best explained with an example. Publius Cornelius Scipio had no son and adopted Lucius Aemilius Paulus, who then took his adopted father's name, Publius Cornelius Scipio. But to show that he was previously a member of the *gens* Aemilia, the name 'Aemilianus' was added, making him Publius Cornelius Scipio Aemilianus (look out for the -*anus* endings on the *gens* to spot these 'adoptive' names). Later when he conquered Carthage, he too was given the name 'Africanus' and so became Publius Cornelius Scipio Africanus Aemilianus. In the late republic and early empire the tendency was for more and more names to be added and the rules were not strictly applied.

In addition to the *trianomina*, an individual's status as a Roman citizen is also indicated by showing his filiation – naming him as the son of his father. So M. Antonius will have been known as M. Antonius M.f. (= *Marci filius*): that is, Marcus Antonius, the son of Marcus, with the father's *praenomen* abbreviated to 'M.' and 'f.' as an abbreviation of *filius* (son). Note that in this example Marcus Antonius only has two names and no *cognomen*, so we can see that a citizen need not always have a *trianomina*. But often the voting tribe of the person was also included in their name (citizens were divided into tribes in order to vote which didn't coincide with *gentes*). So M. Tullius M.f. Cor. Cicero belonged to the Cor(nelia *tribu*) – the Cornelius tribe.

Women were named with the feminine form of the *gens* to which their father belonged. So the daughter of M. Tullius M.f. Cor. Cicero was simply 'Tullia' or 'Tullia M.f.' to distinguish her from other daughters in the same *gens*. Sometimes a married woman might take the feminine form of her husband's *praenomen* as a first name; for example, Gaia would be the wife of

Gaius. Sometimes she might also keep the name derived from her father's *gens*, so Aula Cornelia would be the wife of Aulus and a daughter of the *gens* Cornelia. (This was reversed in the early empire when the same woman would have been called Cornelia Aula.) During the empire the *praenomen* fell out of use and women regularly had two names derived from the *nomen* and *cognomen* of their father, such as Caecilia Metella (the daughter of Caecilius Metellus), or derived from the *nomina* of her father *and* mother, such as Valeria Attia (the daughter of Valeria and Attius).

Slaves usually were given just one name, often Greek in origin, such as Eros or Croesus. But they might be further identified by reference to their master so that Dama L. Titi ser was Dama, slave of Lucius Titius (slave is abbreviated to *ser* for *servus*). Slaves had no *praenomen*, *nomen* or *cognomen*. When a slave was freed and given citizenship they would take the *praenomen* and *nomen* of their ex-master and then their slave name as a new *cognomen*, so that Dama would have become Lucius Titius Dama. Their status as 'freed' would also be indicated in a similar way to filiation: showing they were a *libertus* (freedman) by using the abbreviation 'l.' or 'lib.' and the *praenomen* of their ex-master, so that Dama would then become Lucius Titius L. l. Dama (the freedman 'l' of Lucius 'L').

Names of foreigners and freeborn provincials were usually used in the form of their individual name with the name of their father in the genitive, so that Tritano Acali was Tritano, son of Acalus. This was often further noted by an 'f.' abbreviation for *filius*, as in Tritano Acali f. When they got citizenship they could choose a *praenomen* and *nomen* and their individual name would become the *cognomen*, as in C. Iulius Acalus f. Tritano. It became usual for new citizens to take their names from the emperor who granted them citizenship, so, for example, Ti.Claudius Optatus most likely received citizenship from an emperor of the Claudian family. The same was usually true for auxiliary soldiers who received citizenship when they retired.

From the early empire onwards the *praenomen* began to fall out of use and ordinary people began to use the *cognomen*. This gradually became the usual individual name as the number of new citizens and freedmen grew, since otherwise all the first sons of someone freed by T.Flavius would end up being called T.Flavius, thereby causing great confusion. So, later, a name such as Flavius Tritano would have become more typical, and he may well have been a citizen without having a *trianomina*.

All of this may sound highly complicated, and it is, but it demonstrates how the names of individuals were closely intertwined with both legal and social status. At the beginning of this subsection, you will recall I said that all members of a *gens* shared the same *nomen* – all the Iulii were called Iulius, and they shared (theoretically as you will see) a male ancestor.

Because of this, a name could suggest personal prestige and reputation derived by association from ancestors in the earlier history of the *gens* and their noble and brave exploits. Understanding how Roman names worked, and their significance, will help you in the next subsections.

Legendary genealogies

In this subsection you are going to examine an article published in an academic journal called *Greece and Rome*. There are four reasons for you to study the article.

1   It will give you the opportunity to work with modern scholarship and look at how it is presented, in particular at how the footnotes work. You will also learn how to use footnotes yourself in your academic writing.

2   The content of the article will build your understanding of the importance of genealogy in the Roman republic and link it to other cultural areas: literature, poetry, art and architecture, and politics.

3   You will be able to examine how an academic argument can be constructed.

4   The article – which was written in 1974 – will be considered in relation to what has been learned by new research since its publication.

Exercise

The article, 'Legendary genealogies in late-republican Rome' by T.P. Wiseman, is reprinted in Reading 3.13 of Readings Book 2.

Read the starting quotation, the first paragraph and footnote 1. What does the footnote do? (Note that '*Suet. DJ*' is an abbreviation of Suetonius Divus Julius – refer to p.xvii of the *OCCC* for a list of Classical abbreviations.)

Discussion

The answer is very straightforward. The footnote provides information about where the quote comes from and when it was made. Here is the Suetonius passage from which the quotation is taken:

> 6. During his quaestorship [69 BC], he made the customary funeral speeches from the Rostra in honour of his aunt Julia and his wife Cornelia; and while eulogizing Julia's maternal and paternal ancestry, did the same for the Caesars too. 'Her mother', he said, 'was a descendant of kings, namely the Marcii

> Reges, a family founded by the Roman King Ancus Marcius; and her father, of gods – since the Julians (of which we Caesars are a branch) reckon descent from the Goddess Venus. Thus Julia's stock can claim both the sanctity of kings, who reign supreme among mortals, and the reverence due to gods, who hold even kings in their power.'
>
> He next married Pompeia, Quintus Pompeius's daughter, who was also Sulla's grand-daughter, but divorced her on suspicion of adultery with Publius Clodius; indeed, so persistent was the rumour of Clodius's having disguised himself as a woman and seduced her at the Feast of the Good Goddess, from which all men are excluded, that the Senate ordered a judicial inquiry into the alleged desecration of these sacred rites.
>
> (Suetonius, *Divus Julius* VI.1)

Footnote 1 does not say who translated the original Latin into English, and the passage above is obviously a different translation of the funeral speech from that given by Wiseman. Perhaps Wiseman translated Suetonius' Latin himself; we cannot be sure because the information is not provided. If footnote 1 were accurately referenced, it would have included the name of the translator. But the world is rarely perfect, and so Wiseman loses a mark or two for his study skills.

Exercise

Now read the first two sentences at the start of the second paragraph of the article and also footnote 2. What does footnote 2 do?

Discussion

The first reference in footnote 2 is to a passage by the Roman historian Livy, a primary source, and it supports the statements in the first sentence concerning Iulus, Ascanius and Aeneas. Here it is:

> I will not discuss the question – for who could affirm for certain so ancient a matter? – whether this boy was Ascanius, or an elder brother, born by Creusa while Ilium yet stood, who accompanied his father when he fled from the city, being the same whom the Julian family call Iulus and claim as the author of their name. This Ascanius, no matter where born, or of what mother – it is agreed in any case that he was Aeneas' son ...
>
> (Livy 1.3.2)

This passage from Livy reflects the doubt expressed by Wiseman in the article.

The second part of the footnote refers to a commentary on the first book of Livy written by R.M. Ogilvie. Commentaries are scholarly discussions of ancient texts. Typically, with histories such as Livy's, they will discuss the credibility and veracity of the source, comparing the text in question with other ancient texts, modern scholarship and other relevant sources and evidence such as archaeological finds. Ogilvie has a page of comment on these lines (Ogilvie, 1965, p.42–43). It is very detailed and there is no need to reproduce all his comments, but a few extracts will give you a flavour of the content. He starts off:

> Livy betrays clearly that he has consulted two sources, one of which maintained the identification of Ascanius and Iulus the ancestor of the *gens Iulia* and another which denied or ignored it. The history of the question can be traced …
>
> (Ogilvie, 1965, p.42)

Ogilvie then discusses evidence from Homer and Virgil. Later he considers the tradition of Ascanius being an ancestor of the founder of Rome saying:

> It was doubtless aided by the family pride of the *gens Iulia*, an Alban family who connected their name with Troy by the equivalence Iulus = Ilos and accordingly claimed that Iulus was another name for Ascanius. This was an old claim, already found in Cato (fr.9 P) …
>
> (Ogilvie, 1965, p.42)

Clearly, Ogilvie's comments support Wiseman's point.

The third part of the footnote refers to a second ancient author, Festus, and quotes the passage in Latin as well. It is not clear why Wiseman quotes the Latin here, but it is probably because Festus is quite an obscure source, not easily available in Latin or English, and so he provides it, hoping to be helpful I suppose (even if it is not translated for us). The Latin says that the Aemilian family (*gens*) 'descended from Ascanius who had two sons, Iulus and Aemylos' (my translation). It therefore tells us where Wiseman got his information for the second sentence.

You will also have noticed that Wiseman uses one footnote for two sentences and collects together three different references. This is good practice, and could even be taken further with a single footnote for each paragraph, providing it is clear enough which reference is supporting which assertion or argument.

It would be tedious for us to work through all of the footnotes in this way, but the function of the footnotes in this article is largely to provide supporting evidence for the information or assertions in the article. Occasionally a footnote provides some further comment or discussion – as in footnote 5 – but in this article such footnotes are rare and they mostly refer to ancient primary sources, with a few references to modern scholarship. Before we leave the footnotes there is a point to observe. This article uses different conventions for referring to other works from those that you should use in your work (these are detailed in the Assignment Book). So the presentation of your footnotes will be different but the function they perform – to support your arguments, information and assertions – should be the same.

Reading the article

In the following exercise you will read the complete article, but a few comments first. As you read the article you need not read all the footnotes; after all, they are put away at the bottom of the page so that they do not interrupt the flow of the text. If, however, some assertion of Wiseman strikes you as contentious, unlikely or particularly significant, it is a good idea to look at the footnote and ask yourself a couple of questions. What sort of reference is used to support it – a primary source or modern scholarship? Does this distinction affect the credibility and authority of Wiseman? Ultimately it is good academic practice to check the original source that Wiseman, or any other writer, uses to support any assertion or argument, but most of the time it is necessary to trust that the scholar has done his or her work well so you don't have to check everything. (Academic journals such as *Greece and Rome* employ academics known as 'referees' whose role is to ensure that the quality is high.) If you are dubious about any of Wiseman's arguments or assertions it is a good idea to check the sources he uses. This could involve visiting specialist libraries, but more and more ancient sources and some modern scholarship in academic journals are now becoming available on the internet. For example, JSTOR, accessible from the course website, is a vast, searchable collection of academic articles, and it contains all the volumes of *Greece and Rome*, including the article you are about to read. (Note that we have reformatted it for reproduction in Readings Book 2 – in the original all the footnotes are numbered starting with one on each separate page.) Both the Suetonius and the Livy sources just referred to can also be found relatively easily on the internet. (At the time of writing Festus is not available, but scholars are working on it. See the eDesktop for links.)

To help you in your reading I have provided a glossary of technical terms not found in the *OCCC*, including Greek and Latin words used in the text. This is printed in Readings Book 2 after the article. I have not provided details of all the names in the text: most of those that are only mentioned once or twice are examples illustrating Wiseman's points, and in truth very little is known about them other than their names and relations. You are certainly not expected to memorise them. Some, like Caesar or Aeneas, you will meet more frequently. If you wish you can look up the names in the *OCCC,* but you will only find the less obscure ones there.

Exercise

Read the complete article in Reading 3.13 about the supposed genealogies of certain Roman families. As you read:

1   Note down the categories of ancestors you encounter: kings, gods etc.

2   Analyse the structure of the article, identifying the major topics discussed and the changes in direction of the subject matter and argument. Try to distil the article down into a list of these topics set out in the order they are discussed.

In effect, I am asking you to work out the plan behind the article, the kind of plan you would start with if you were writing an essay. Please do this, because after reading the article we will be analysing the plan and its logic to see how persuasive Wiseman is. We will also hold the article to question against the advances in scholarship in the thirty years since it was written.

Colour Plates 12–15 in the Illustrations Book and Figures 3.7 and 3.8 below provide illustrations for the article.

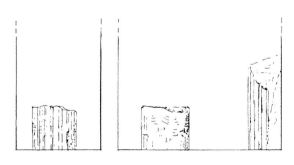

Figure 3.7   Elevation of the remains of the Temple of Mars in Circo, from Ernest Nash, *Pictorial Dictionary of Ancient Rome Vol. II*, Thames and Hudson, 1968, pl. 832, p.121. © Ernst Wasmuth Verlag, D-72072 Tübingen, Germany.

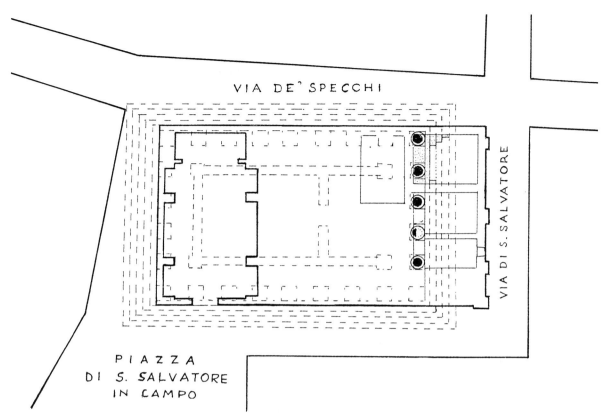

Figure 3.8   Plan of the remains of the Temple of Mars in Circo (dashed line) and the Church of San Salvatore in Campo (solid line), from Ernest Nash, *Pictorial Dictionary of Ancient Rome Vol. II*, Thames and Hudson, 1968, pl. 833, p.121. © Ernst Wasmuth Verlag, D-72072 Tübingen, Germany.

Discussion

Wiseman's essay has four main parts.

1   The first part (up to 'But was that how it appeared to contemporaries?') provides a dazzling and somewhat bewildering range of examples of Roman families claiming descent from mythical figures, especially Trojans who escaped the sack of Troy. The details may pass us by, but it appears clear that the Roman élite was very interested in the possibility of having divine or heroic ancestors.

What do you think about the amount of material in this section? Could the overall point have been made more economically? We might be impressed by the long list of families and their mythical bloodlines, but the important points – that élite Roman families claimed descent from deities, legendary figures and literary heroes to enhance their own prestige – could have been made in a much more straightforward way. Simply asserting that this is what they did and then providing a single, good example of each main type of descent line (gods, heroes, founders of cities and Trojans), with supporting footnotes to substantiate the claims, would probably be enough. However, I think that the final two sentences of this section are a good link to the next section. Wiseman quotes a modern scholar Ronald Syme, one of the most influential historians of the Roman republic in the twentieth century, and the quotation comes from his best-known work. Wiseman then questions whether this authoritative historian was correct in his judgement. It is a good quotation to choose because it is rather extreme and does not mince its words. And it is used to ask what the Romans themselves would have thought about the genealogies. This shift of focus enables Wiseman to then go on to discuss a new range of ancient sources that contrast with those he has already discussed.

2   The second part (up to 'There is, I think, one splendid example which has not been recognized for what it is') addresses the historical (or ahistorical) nature of the genealogies with reference to both Roman historians and the audience who would have heard about the genealogies. This establishes that the good and prestigious story was more important that the historical truth. Wiseman achieves this by citing sources that question the veracity of the claimed genealogies. He discusses some interesting ancient opinions on history ('the true', 'the seeming-true' and 'the false'). I think this is a strong section, but I do think he ducks the issue a bit by deciding that it does not really matter whether the genealogies were considered true or false because what matters is that they were devised as impressive entertaining stories. Surely impressive entertaining stories can also be true, seemingly-true, and false.

The link to the third section, the last paragraph in the second section, is, I think, rather rushed and does not carefully explain what it means. What Wiseman is trying to achieve is a shift in his discussion of genealogy and history from the written to the visual and archaeological evidence. The paragraph jumps from coins to sculpture to propaganda to temples, finally ending up with Greeks. This paragraph seems too compressed and Wiseman should have explained more carefully how each of these topics related to his argument. It is not the case that he is wrong; he just does not explain himself clearly enough. The last sentence of this paragraph reveals why Wiseman has written a rather bumpy linking paragraph: he is joining his previous discussion to a splendid and interesting case-study that he wants to write about (at length).

3   In the next section (up to the end of the paragraph ending 'the legendary genealogy of the censor's family'), Wiseman introduces an archaeological find – the relief sculptures – and contextualises them, claiming that they relate to his discussion of genealogy. He then briefly dismisses two rival explanations by saying that the description of the Temple of Neptune as *in circo* is inappropriate to the find spot of the remains, and that the secondary location of Neptune on the reliefs was not appropriate for a representation of the god in his own temple. In fact, Wiseman has already sown the seeds of this rejection in the first paragraph of the third section where he refers to the temple as 'an unidentified Roman temple'.

In this section Wiseman is clearly writing about something that he finds interesting – as indeed it is – but I feel that his writing becomes too narrative. He is telling us everything that he has been able to find out about the temple and the reliefs, and I believe he rather loses sight of the subject in question – the genealogies – given the fact that the title of the essay is 'Legendary genealogies in late-republican Rome'. It is a few paragraphs later that he returns to the point; and even then he makes the rather weak link that the fact that the relief shows a marriage (does it?) means that it relates to genealogy. (A scene from the Trojan War might be more convincing.) Perhaps he might have used a slightly different title: something like 'Legendary genealogies in late-republican Rome and the reliefs of the so-called altar of Domitius Ahenobarbus'. More of a mouthful perhaps, but he could not then be accused of deviating from the title of the essay.

4   From the paragraph beginning 'Of the sixteen censors ...', Wiseman rejects previous identifications of the provider of the reliefs and this serves as an introduction to the final section in which he puts forward his favoured solution. So here we reach the culmination of the essay, where Wiseman provides his own thoughts and his own interpretation of the evidence he has been discussing. I'd say this is a good way to end an essay.

His final explanation and interpretation is based on the following arguments:

(a) that the relief depicts a censor sacrificing;

(b) that most of the censors may be rejected as possible benefactors because they either had different genealogies or no known mythological genealogy;

(c) that a mythological genealogical link can be made between the censor L. Gellius and Neptune.

These three reasons are enough for Wiseman to suggest that he has established which censor is celebrated in the relief panels. However, he does not trumpet his conclusion. In the penultimate paragraph but one, he concludes in general terms that: 'It shows us how a Roman statesman, and one thoroughly imbued with his ancestral traditions, wished to project himself to the people of Rome ...', before ending with another general flourish: 'With a god in the family tree, who needed consuls?' This appears to be a final attempt to get back to the point of the essay, which he has come very close to wandering away from in his discussion of the reliefs.

Exercise

How convinced are you by Wiseman's identification of L. Gellius as the man in the relief and therefore presumably the benefactor of the temple? Write down the reasons why you are convinced, or not convinced, or uncertain, based on what you have read.

Discussion

If you are convinced you may have noted the following:

1 Wiseman's case is well argued, coherent and convincing.

2 He refers to the work of Kähler and Coarelli to support the identification of the censor.

3 He provides reasons why the other possible censors could not have been represented with Neptune.

4 He establishes a link between Neptune and the Gellii.

5 He's a well-respected Classical scholar and the article is published in a reputable journal.

If you aren't convinced you may have noted the following:

1 The argument is difficult to follow: it seems rather tortuous and not particularly focused on solving the problem.

2 Wiseman's reasons for rejecting the other censors are unconvincing because although some have different known

mythical genealogies, to argue the others did not, simply because none are known in the surviving source, is not sufficient proof – and he doesn't explicitly reject M. Perperna for any reason.

3   The link between the Gellii and Neptune is tenuous: it depends on linking their tribe, the Tromentina, to a particular area and a later Gellius known from a nearby city. The tribe, however, may also have been found elsewhere. There is also a dubious and obscure link between Lamus, the son of Neptune, his daughter Lamia (also known as Gello) and the Gellii.

4   It is a bit too convenient that the solution to this particular problem lies in the main topic of the paper – mythological genealogies. Which came first? Wiseman's identification of the problem in being sure who is represented on the relief, or his interest in the genealogies? I suspect the latter.

5   I am naturally very sceptical and none of Wiseman's arguments were sufficient to convince me that he *must* be right.

If you are uncertain you may have noted the following:

1   None of Wiseman's arguments were strong enough to convince me that he is right and he didn't provide me with enough reasons why the other scholars were wrong.

2   He did not consider the possibility that the relief did not represent a censor.

3   I don't feel that Wiseman has got to the bottom of this. I would like more information before I decide whether or not I think he is right or wrong.

4   Why is all the focus on Neptune when the man making the sacrifice is standing next to Mars?

You may have come up with other reasons. But whatever you concluded, I hope that by noting some of the possible flaws and strengths in the arguments I have made, you reflect upon why you came to your decision about whether you found Wiseman convincing. If not, think about it again now that I have presented you with conflicting notes. Do you want to change your mind?

Advances in scholarship after Wiseman

Wiseman's article was published in 1974, and since then a number of other scholars have studied and written about the temple and the reliefs. I wonder if Wiseman would now wish to change his mind about the identification of the temple and its patron. There is still no unanimous agreement, but a strong alternative possibility was put forward by Fausto Zevi (1976). He realised that it was not actually certain that the reliefs belonged to the temple and came to the same conclusion as Wiseman that the temple was not the Temple of Neptune. Furthermore, a surviving representation of the Temple of Neptune on a coin minted by Cn. Domitius L.f. Ahenobarbus in 42/1 BCE (Figure 3.9) had only four columns on the front, whereas the remains under the church indicated a temple with six columns on the front. The fragmentary remains of the temple indicate that it was of a Greek type with columns set upon steps that ran all around the temple and that it was built of Greek white marble (Figures 3.7 and 3.8). Now a passage by the Roman author Cornelius Nepos states that the Temple of Mars lay in the Circus Flaminius and was built by Hermodorus of Salamis (Platner and Ashby, 1926, p.328). In addition, a fragment of the marble plan of Rome, showing a Hellenistic temple with columns all around, can also be matched to the location near the circus of Flaminius, and finally a statue of seated Mars was also found in the area in the 1600s. The combination of the written and archaeological sources, together with the uncommon Greek style of the temple, creates a strong case for the remains being the Temple of Mars. This identification means that the Temple of Neptune needs to be located elsewhere – so what about those sculptures?

Figure 3.9   Coin of Cn. Domitius L.f. Ahenobarbus, depicting the Temple of Neptune, 42/1 BCE. British Museum, London. Photo: © The Trustees of The British Museum.

Zevi claims that he can interpret the reliefs with reference to the man who founded the Temple of Mars (D. Iunius Brutus Callaicus) after a victory over the Gallicians in the extreme west of Spain (Valerius Maximus 8.3.1). The Iunii claimed descent from a Trojan, but also from Lucius Iunius Brutus, the semi-legendary founder of the Roman republic, who expelled Tarquinius Superbus (the last King of Rome, whom you met at the beginning of Section 2.4). Lucius Iunius Brutus consecrated his lands to Mars, and created the Campus Martius, in the heart of which lay the Circus of Flaminius. So, according to Zevi, this is the act that the sacrifice in the reliefs refers to, and the marriage of Neptune refers to D.Iunius Brutus Callaicus' victory over distant people living next to the ocean. The latter does not seem a very strong argument in my view: we see another tenuous connection and there is no trace of victory celebrations in the reliefs. Still, Zevi doesn't insist that the reliefs belong to the temple so his identification isn't undermined. Interestingly, if we were to accept Zevi's analysis, it could still fit with the general topic of Wiseman's essay since Zevi, too, believes that the commemoration of ancestors in public benefaction was a significant event for the Roman élite.

In 1982, Mario Torelli wrote in partial disagreement with Zevi in a book about historical reliefs. He accepted the identification of the Temple of Mars but rejected the interpretation of the frieze, preferring to emphasise the scenes relating to the wedding of Poseidon and Amphitrite and relate them to the Temple of Neptune in Circo. He hypothesised that the Temple of Neptune lies along side the Temple of Mars and the reliefs formed the base for a set of statues offered to Neptune (Torelli, 1982, pp.5–9). He goes on to interpret the scene on the fourth side thus. On the left, there are scenes from the census where a citizen's details and wealth are recorded and he is then assigned to a class of citizens, who are represented by the horseman on the right, an *eques*, and the other foot soldiers representing the lower classes of citizens. In the centre is the sacrifice that forms part of a lustrum – a ritual purification of the classes defined as a result of the census (Torelli, 1982, pp.9–14). He then dates the reliefs by relating the similar arms of the soldiers to the fact that in 123 BCE a law passed by C.Gracchus provided for arms to be supplied to citizens by the state, giving an earliest possible date, and finding a latest possible date by stating that the classes of soldiers represented ceased to exist after the army was reformed in 107 BCE. This leads him to identify Cn. Domitius Ahenobarbus as the censor (in 115 BCE) who dedicated the reliefs (Torelli, 1982, pp.14–16). So, according to Torelli, the so-called altar of Domitius Ahenobarbus is not an altar at all, but it was dedicated by Ahenobarbus.

In 1997, Fillipo Coarelli revisited the problem with the benefit of some new discoveries and provided a revised interpretation. He still agreed with Zevi that the Temple of Mars lies beneath the Church of San Salvatore in

Campo, but suggested that it is possible that the reliefs were not found there. This contradicts the conclusion of Coarelli's earlier work which stated that they *were* found there and which Wiseman unwisely described as 'brilliant archival detective-work' (Reading 3.13). Instead, further archival work suggests that they may have been found elsewhere along with a statue representing Achilles. This discovery, along with the finding of a second century BCE capital from a temple in the basement of the house built in CE 1497 by Lorenzo Manilio, enabled Coarelli to suggest that this was the location of the Temple of Neptune alongside the Circus of Flaminius rather than a site immediately beside the Temple of Mars. Coarelli then attached to his hypothesis a passage from Pliny the Elder that describes a group of statues said by Pliny to have been made by a famous Greek sculptor, Skopas:

> But most highly esteemed of all his works is the group in the temple built by Gnaeus Domitius in the Circus of Flaminius: it comprises Poseidon himself with Thetis and Achilles, Nereids riding on dolphins and sea monsters or on sea horses, and Tritons and the train of Phorkos with sea beasts and many other sea animalsa tumult of creatures of the deep, the whole by the same hand, a wondrous work, even were it that of a life-time.
>
> (Pliny, *Natural History* 36.26)

Coarelli suggests that Pliny is describing three statues on a base decorated with sea scenes which can be identified with the so-called altar of Domitius Ahenobarbus (Colour Plates 12–15 in your Illustrations Book). So far so good – but Coarelli has no strong explanation for why the census is represented, suggesting that it may have been added to the sea scenes following Cn. Domitius Ahenobarbus' spell as censor to commemorate his ancestor Cn. Domitius Calvinus Maximus, the first plebian to hold the rank of censor in 280 BCE.

The argument continues and the most recent book-length study of the reliefs by Florian (Stilp, 2001) treats them without relating them to the Temple of Mars at all, preferring that they should be associated with the Temple of Neptune which lies somewhere nearby. Furthermore, the suggestion that the man offering the sacrifice can be identified is rejected and the scene is interpreted as representing the Roman concept of *pietas* (piety or the performance of religious duty). This will not be the last word on the subject, and Stilp lists over 200 earlier works that have discussed the reliefs. In 2002, Peter Holliday discussed the reliefs, making some detailed observations, but prefers to identify them as a monument to the sea triumph of Marcus Antonius censor in 97 BCE, without refuting the previous suggestions (Holliday, 2002, p.162). So why have the reliefs received such attention?

Exercise

Look at Colour Plate 14, the census relief, in the Illustrations Book. You already know a great deal about its context – even if there is no certainty about where it was found. Examine the details of what the figures are doing. What, at the broadest level, is represented? (Don't describe the detail: think about what it is representing as a whole and encapsulate it in a few words.)

Discussion

If you said a sacrifice and related (census) activity, you are right. But at an even more general level it is a relief representing a historical event: the sacrifice and the associated census. This is why it is important. It is the earliest Roman representation of a historical event in sculpture (even if there is a god taking part and its date is not precisely known). This is the principal reason why the reliefs have received so much attention: they lie at the beginning of a Roman tradition of representing historical events as a frieze which will include monuments such as the Ara Pacis, commemorating Augustus' achievement of peace after the Civil Wars, and Trajan's Column, representing his conquest of Dacia. The broader art-historical significance of these reliefs overshadows their architectural, mythological or historical significance, and this is probably why Wiseman was interested in them in the first place.

You could also take an even wider view of their place in art history by comparing them, and what you have learned about them, with the Parthenon reliefs, and the debates surrounding them.

Making and leaving your mark

So far in this section you have studied how reputations could be established through military and political achievements or divine associations. These reputations are recorded in literature, in family tombs, or immortalised in stone in a relief, or by the dedication of a temple. In this final subsection we will look more closely at temple building as a means of establishing and communicating a reputation. The primary function of a temple was religious: it provided a home for a god and a focus for cult practices. Chapter 3 of Beard and Crawford discusses issues concerning how Roman religion can be studied and its role in Roman public life. If you have time, you could read it now, but it is not necessary to do so for the purposes of our current focus on how temple building was used to record dynastic achievements.

In the Wiseman article you have already learned that a successful politician could use art and architecture (e.g. reliefs in a temple) to celebrate his achievements and indulge in self-advertisement to enhance his status. The same motivations could also be incorporated into a religious context through a grander and more serious undertaking – dedicating an entire temple. We have seen how a god or goddess might be one of the family as a remote ancestor; or how an individual such as Pompey might have a personal relationship with a goddess like Venus, and how Lucius Cornelius Scipio son of Lucius dedicated a temple to the storm god. Divine intervention could also be called for in times of desperate need. Beard and Crawford (pp.30–31) outline a view that Roman religion was both a public religion and that the gods took a part in promoting the success of the Roman state. Furthermore, they state that: 'The Romans saw the interests of their state as served by military victory – and those interests were necessarily upheld by the gods. Divine support combined with the prowess of the soldiers to increase the power of Rome' (Beard and Crawford, p.31). So much the better then if one's own reputation could be associated with divinely-aided support for the state.

The combination of divinity, victory and personal prestige lies behind much of the debate surrounding the census reliefs: for example, Zevi's theory that they commemorate D. Iunius Brutus Callaicus' victory over the Gallicians, or Holliday's that the sea triumph of Marcus Antonius was the inspiration. The same combination of factors also transformed the fabric of the city of Rome as victorious, divinely-inspired generals dedicated new temples in thanks for the victories of the expanding republic. A victorious general could dispose of war booty in any way he wished, and much of this was spent building temples to commemorate great victories. These temples (known as 'victory temples') became, in effect, monuments to the glory of the victorious general and his family. The temples tended to cluster around the Circus Flaminius, the area where triumphal processions started, and along the route the processions took, via the Roman forum to the Capitoline hill. Unfortunately, none of these temples survive in their entirety, but it is possible to identify some of their remains and some of their locations in areas that have not been excavated.

Exercise

Watch DVD3, Section 3, 'The *Campus Martius*'. The DVD ties together several themes of the block. As you watch, note down the themes or topics that you have studied so far as they crop up. Figures 3.10–14 provide maps and plans of the area under consideration in the DVD and they will help you to become familiar with the topography of this part of the city of Rome.

Discussion

The DVD ties together some aspects of the political organisation of Rome with the physical remains of the city. The commentary identifies some of the locations of political events. Throughout, the buildings are related to the men who paid for their construction. Often they are temples constructed following a vow made in the heat of battle. These temples therefore commemorate the achievements of great men, and simultaneously demonstrate how the political and military successes of the republic are overseen by the gods. Personal glory, public fame and religious duty are all bound together in the structures of the city. Buildings were used to enhance personal reputation as well as to commemorate the achievements of ancestors.

Another theme that emerges is the intermingling of Greek and Roman architecture. Ties between Greek and Roman culture are emphasised at several points. The DVD visits the sites of the Temples of Mars and Neptune although there is nothing to be seen of the temples. The detailed studies of some of the buildings (such as the Porticus of Octavia or the temples in Largo Argentina) illustrate the complexity of the archaeological remains and the intricacies involved in interpreting the evidence. If the Temples of Mars and Neptune were ever to be excavated their remains would be just as complex, and the new evidence would fuel academic debate even more.

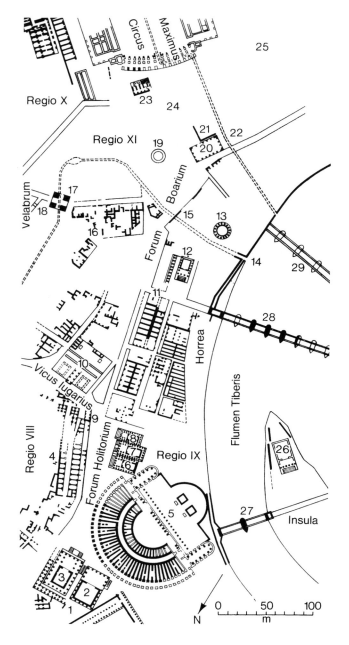

1 Porticus of Octavia	11 Porta Flumentana	21 Great Altar of Hercules
2 Temple of Apollo Medicus Sosianus	12 Temple of Portunus	22 Porta Trigemina
3 Temple of Bellona	13 Temple of Hercules Olivarius	23 Mithraeum
4 ?Porticus Triumphi	14 Cloaca Maxima	24 Temple of Hercules Pompeianus
5 Theatre of Marcellus	15 Republican walls	25 Temple of Ceres
6 Temple of Janus	16 Imperial buildings	26 Temple of Aesculapius
7 Temple of Juno Sospita	17 Arch of Janus	27 Pons Fabricius
8 Temple of Spes	18 Arch of the Argentarii	28 Pons Aemilianus (Ponte Rotto)
9 Porta Carmentalis	19 Temple of Hercules Aemilianus	29 Pons Sublicius
10 Temples of Fortuna and Mater Matuta	20 Porticus of Santa Maria in Cosmedin	

Figure 3.10   Plan of the Forum Holitorium (vegetable market) and Forum Boarium (cattlemarket) districts, by the River Tiber, Rome. From Filippo Coarelli, *Roma*, terza edizione, Roma-Bari: Gius. Laterza & Figli Spa, 2003, p.379.

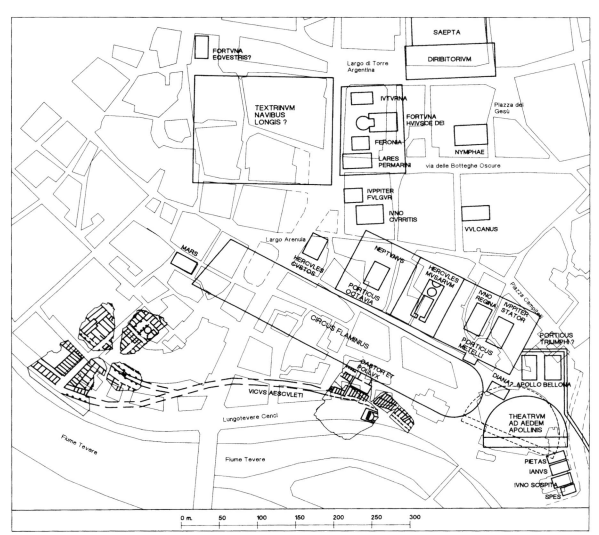

Figure 3.11   The area of the Circus Flaminius and the central Campus Martius from Filippo Coarelli, *Il Campo Marzio dalle origini alla fine della repubblica*, Rome: Edizioni Quasar, 1997, p.364. The imperial period walls known from the marble plan are marked in black. Note that the plans and identifications of many of these buildings are only hypotheses. Temples are identified only by the names of the deities.

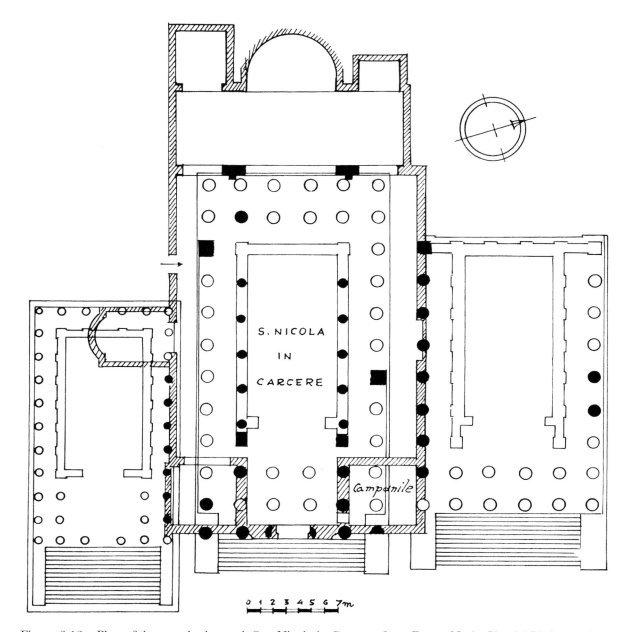

Figure 3.12   Plan of the temples beneath San Nicola in Carcere, from Ernest Nash, *Pictorial Dictionary of Ancient Rome Vol. 1*, revised ed., London: Thames and Hudson, 1968, fig. 512, p.419. © Ernst Wasmuth Verlag, D-72072 Tübingen, Germany. The church is overlaid in hatched lines. Surviving standing columns are shown in black. Left to right: Temple of Spes, Temple of Juno Sospita, Temple of Janus.

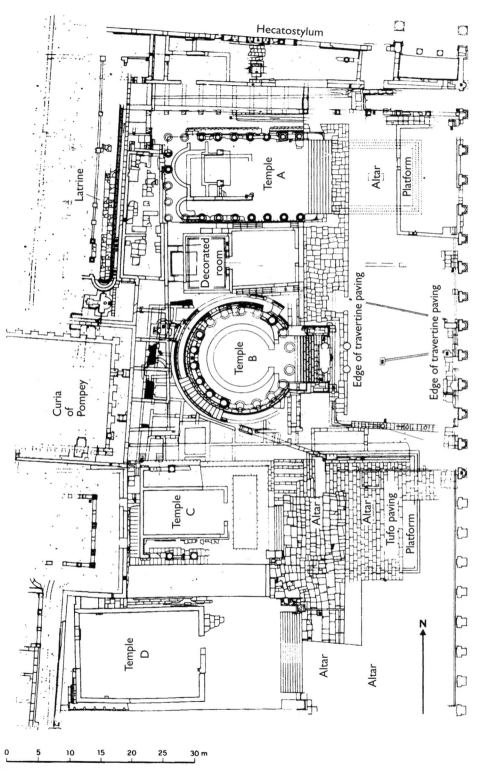

Figure 3.13 Plan of the temples in the Largo Argentina Sacred Area, from Filippo Coarelli, *Roma*, terza edizione, Roma-Bari: Gius. Laterza & Figli Spa, 2003, p.334.

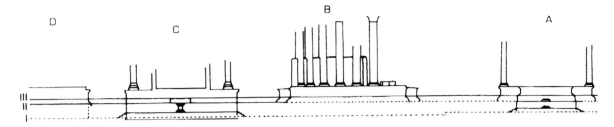

Figure 3.14   Elevations of the temples in the Largo Argentina Sacred Area, from Filippo Coarelli, *Roma*, terza edizione, Roma-Bari: Gius. Laterza & Figli Spa, 2003, p.335. The drawing shows successive levels of paving: I = original level, II = republican level, III = Domitianic level. The letters identify the temples.

References

Ancient sources

Livy, *Natural History*, in B.O. Foster (trans.) (1976) *Livy in Fourteen Volumes*, vol.1, books I and II, London: Heinemann.

Martial, *Epigrams* 8.30, in Anon (trans.) (1909) *The Epigrams of Martial*, George Bell and Sons.

Pliny the Elder, *Natural History* 36.26, in K. Jex-Blake (trans.) (1982) *The Elder Pliny's Chapters on the History of Art*, Chicago: Ares.

Pliny the Elder, *Natural History* 7.139–40, in T.P. Wiseman (trans.) (1985) *Roman Political Life 90 BC–69 AD*, Exeter: University of Exeter, Exeter Studies in History no.7.

Suetonius, *Divus Julius* VI.1, in R. Graves (trans.) (1980) *Gaius Seutonius Tranquillus: The Twelve Caesars*, London: Penguin.

Valerius Maximus, *Memorable Doings and Sayings* 8.3.1, in D.R. Shackleton-Bailey (trans.) (2000) *Valerius Maximus: Memorable Doings and Sayings*, Cambridge, MA: Harvard University Press.

Modern scholarship

Bodel, J. (ed.) (2001) *Epigraphic Evidence: Ancient History from Inscriptions*, London: Routledge.

Chaplin, J.D. (2000) *Livy's Exemplary History*, Oxford: Oxford University Press.

Coarelli, F. (1997) *Il Campo Marzio, dalle origini alla fine della repubblica*, Rome: Edizioni Quasar.

Holliday, P.J. (2002) *The Origins of Roman Historical Commemoration in the Visual Arts*, Cambridge: Cambridge University Press.

Mouritsen, H. (2001) *Plebs and Politics in the Late Roman Republic*, Cambridge: Cambridge University Press.

Ogilvie, R.M. (1965) *A Commentary on Livy: Books 1–5*, Oxford: Clarendon Press.

Platner, S.B and Ashby, T. (1926) *A Topographical Dictionary of Rome*, Oxford: Oxford University Press.

Stilp, F. (2001) *Mariage et Suovetaurlia: Etude sur le Soi-disant 'Autel Ahenobarbus'*, RdA Supplementi 26, Rome: Giorgio di Bretschneider.

Torelli, M. (1982) *Typology and Structure of Roman Historical Reliefs*, Ann Arbor: University of Michigan Press.

Wiseman, T.P. (1985) *Roman Political Life 90 BC–69 AD*, Exeter: University of Exeter, Exeter Studies in History no.7.

Zevi, F. (1976) 'L'identificazione del tempio di Marte "in circo" e altre osservazioni', in *Melanges J. Heuergon II*, pp.1047–64.

Further reading

Bodel, J. (2001) *Epigraphic Evidence: Ancient History from Inscriptions*, London: Routledge.

Chaplin, J.D. (2000) *Livy's Exemplary History*, Oxford: Oxford University Press.

Claridge, A. (1998) *Rome: An Oxford Archaeological Guide*, Oxford: Oxford University Press.

Part 4 Land, people and power

4.1 The Gracchi brothers

If Cato, the Cornelii, and all the other members of the Roman élite who wished to perpetuate their achievements represented tradition and Rome's ancestral customs (*mos maiorum*), the Gracchi brothers – to whom we now turn our attention – represented the opposite extreme. The careers of these two brothers show up the fault lines that were developing in Roman politics: I am sure you will have noticed the level of competition and some of the tensions that had been building up during this period. But before we look at why the Gracchi brothers are so important historically, let us first consider their background.

The Gracchi brothers were from a distinguished and noble family. Their father had a notable military career: he primarily saw service as governor of Spain and reached the consulship twice (in 177 and 163 BCE), as well as holding the censorship in between these periods of office. His name was Tiberius Gracchus, or, to give him his full *trianomina*, Tiberius Sempronius Gracchus. (As you learned in Section 2.3, it was common for an eldest son to have the same name as his father.) Their mother was Cornelia and she was the daughter of no less a figure than Scipio Africanus, conqueror of Hannibal. Cornelia bore twelve children, only three of whom survived into adulthood. These were the two brothers Tiberius and Gaius and their sister Sempronia. When their father died in 154 BCE, Tiberius was about twelve years old and his brother Gaius only two. Even though she had so many children, Cornelia was widowed at quite a young age. She refused all offers of remarriage and brought up her children alone, giving them a famously liberal education. She had a reputation for being something of a *philhellene*, or admirer of Greek culture, and the education of her sons was therefore along Greek lines. Cornelia remained famous throughout Roman history, and was primarily remembered as 'the mother of the Gracchi': she was thought to represent a certain type of virtuous Roman matron. There are no portraits of Cornelia despite her celebrity, but after her death a statue of her was erected. Pliny the Elder describes it in his *Natural History*, noting that 'This statue which represents her as seated is unusual in that it has sandals which have no strap ...' (Pliny, 34.31). Many anecdotes from her life were known. Valerius Maximus, a writer of the first century CE, recorded the following story in his *Memorable Deeds and Sayings*. When another woman who was a guest in her house 'showed her jewellery the finest in existence at that period, Cornelia kept her in talk until her children came home from school, and then said "These are my jewels".' (*Memorabilia* 4.4).

Exercise

Look at Figure 3.15 below and answer these questions:

- Which myth is being represented?
- Who is the character standing to the left?

If you need some help in finding out the answers, go to 'Course links Block 3' on the course website and use the resources there to aid you.

Figure 3.15   Silver denarius of Sextus Pompeius Fostlus (reverse), showing a wolf and twins, which dates to the time of the Gracchi (*c.*140 BCE). British Museum, London, BMC926 PCR 89. © Copyright The Trustees of the British Museum.

Discussion

I expect that you recognised this image pretty easily, as this particular myth is still well-known today. The coin shows Romulus and his brother Remus being suckled by a she-wolf. You may have done a little research to find out that the figure standing to the left is the shepherd Faustulus. The depiction of the she-wolf is interesting; her hackles are raised and she has large fearsome jaws, but she is also licking the babies and standing over them protectively while they feed. She is Rome; powerful and potentially dangerous, yet protective and nurturing. (See Plate 41 in the Illustrations Book showing the bronze statue of Lupa Romana.)

Tiberius Gracchus

Read the entry for 'Gracchus, Tiberius' in the *OCCC*. Then read the
first part of the section entitled 'A descriptive framework' in Beard and
Crawford, Chapter One, 'The Nature of the Problem', pp.4–6. Write
a paragraph in answer to the following question:

- What problems was Tiberius Gracchus seeking to address and
  what caused them?

Discussion

You probably didn't find this too difficult, as it largely consolidates
work we have already done. The basic problem that Tiberius sought
to remedy – according to these secondary sources – was the
decreasing number of small citizen farmers and the lack of recruits for
the army which this caused. A corollary problem was that there were
too many slaves flooding onto the market. As we have seen, small
farmers were leaving the land for a range of reasons, thus making
themselves ineligible for military service. We have already touched on
the reasons why this occurred: extended military service meant that
small farmers were unable to bring their land back into production
when they returned (many, of course, were also killed during Rome's
wars). On top of that, growing grain became less profitable due to
increasing imports from the provinces, especially Sicily and Africa.
There was a move toward crops which required more investment,
such as olives, and grapes for the production of wine. There was
generally more money around, especially for the élite who wanted to
buy land to form larger more profitable estates, which they could then
work with slave labour.

Exercise

Read the passages from the *OCCC* and Beard and Crawford a second
time. This time note down how Tiberius sought to remedy these
problems. Think about which group of people were most likely to lose
out by his proposals.

Discussion

The solution that Tiberius arrived at might have struck you as rather
oblique. The policy he proposed was essentially one of land
redistribution, and the land he targeted was the *ager publicus* held above

the legal limit of 500 *iugera* (approximately 125 hectares). The land reclaimed for the state in this process would then be redistributed to poor citizen farmers, often by the establishment of colonies.

You have already studied the colony of Paestum in DVD3, Section 1. You may wish to review the parts where attention was focused on the city itself – a city which in some ways became a miniature reproduction of the city of Rome, with an analogous range of public and sacred buildings and monuments. Meanwhile, in the countryside around Paestum, it is possible to trace how the establishment of the Roman city was paralleled by the division of the countryside into regular plots that were assigned to the colonists so that they could farm the land and support themselves in the new territory. This allotment of land would have caused the displacement of the previous owners – whether Greeks or the defeated Lucanians – and the installation of new landowners. Evidence from the landscape around Paestum indicated that the land to the north and east of the city was divided into strips, parts of which would have been assigned to each citizen-colonist, establishing a landscape of small landholdings around the city.

By the time of Tiberius Gracchus, 140 years after the foundation of Paestum, the size of such allotments appears to have been 30 *iugera*, which was considered ample to support a family. This perhaps puts into perspective how much 500 *iugera* really was. To facilitate the redistribution of public land Tiberius Gracchus sought to establish a three-man land commission which would look into holdings of *ager publicus* and decide how much should be confiscated. By these measures he hoped to create more small farmers and thus more potential manpower for the Roman army. Who was most likely to lose out by these proposals? Well, anyone who held more than the legal limit of public land. Many members of the Roman élite clearly stood to lose out, but there is also a suggestion in our sources (Beard and Crawford, p.82) that non-citizen Italian landowners were farming *ager publicus*.

Once again, we need to ask where this information in the secondary sources comes from. To help you understand how this process works, we shall now look at an ancient source and you should be able to see exactly how ancient sources are used by modern historians to produce a secondary account of these events.

Exercise

Now read Appian 1.9–10 in Reading 3.14. As you read, note down any areas where the ancient source gives a different emphasis or where it introduces new information from what you have already learned. Consider whether or not the élite were justified in their complaints about the proposals. What were their main arguments against it?

Do you feel that you have gained a better understanding of these events than you had by just reading the secondary sources?

Discussion

Because you already had some knowledge of these events you should not have found understanding this extract too difficult. There is some new information here: for example, Appian puts quite a lot of stress on Tiberius Gracchus' concern for the Italian allies and also mentions the serious slave revolt that broke out in Sicily in 135 BCE and lasted until 132. These slave revolts were traumatic events for the Romans and there were several that were serious. In the first Sicilian revolt an army composed of perhaps 70,000 escaped slaves was formed, which defeated a number of Roman armies sent against it. The last revolt (73–71 BCE) was famously led by a trainee gladiator from Thrace named Spartacus.

In terms of Tiberius Gracchus' legislation, Appian mentions that the confiscated public land given to poor citizens could not be sold. He also tells us that the children of those with excess holdings of public land would be able to keep 250 *iugera* for each child up to a maximum of an additional 500 *iugera*. It would be easy to conclude that the rich landowners were simply being greedy, but Appian lists some of their detailed complaints, which are very interesting. They argued that they had improved this land, by cultivating it, planting crops and erecting buildings. It had formed part of dowries and been used as collateral for loans. So even though you can probably sympathise with the poorer citizens, who had fought and risked their lives in the wars which won this public land, and had ended up with none of the rewards, you can perhaps also understand how the propertied classes felt that their family land was being stolen from them. You may have felt that there is more colour in this ancient account than in the secondary sources.

A good historian will look at as much ancient evidence as possible in order to ascertain where there is agreement between sources and perhaps also where they differ. In that spirit, we're now going to look at Plutarch's account of these same events.

Contemporary views of Tiberius Gracchus' reforms

Exercise

Read Plutarch's 'Tiberius Gracchus' 9 in Reading 3.15 (a).

1   Does this account add anything that we do not already know?

2   Which side do you think Plutarch sympathises with most?

3   What comments might we make about Tiberius Gracchus' speech at the end of the extract?

Discussion

1   Plutarch tells us that Tiberius Gracchus' scheme had powerful backing from certain members of the senatorial élite, including one of that year's consuls as well as the *pontifex maximus* (Rome's chief priest) and Tiberius' father-in-law Appius Claudius. These powerful and élite voices tell us something very important: that the senate was not united in opposition to these reforms. Though both accounts do suggest that there was formidable opposition, the spectre of revolution was raised in order to undermine support for the new law. His opponents were able to claim that Tiberius was seeking to make himself a tyrant – a tyrant in the Greek sense of 'unconstitutional ruler' rather than the pejorative meaning the term has now. They would be able to use his liberal 'Greek-style' education to suggest that he was tainted with un-Roman ideas; a man whose motives were not to be trusted.

2   I expect you decided that Plutarch seems to be firmly on the side of the poorer citizens. It is interesting how he puts the case rather differently from Appian: he leaves out arguments against the proposal. He also gives us a wonderful little piece of oratory at the end of the passage. We should assume that he has made up this speech and put it into the mouth of Tiberius – a common practice among ancient historians and expected of them. Thucydides puts it thus:

In this history I have made use of set speeches some of which were delivered just before and others during the war. I have found it difficult to remember the precise words used in the speeches which I listened to myself and my various informants have experienced the same difficulty; so my method has been, while keeping as closely as possible to the general sense of the words that were actually used, to make the speakers say what, in my opinion, was called for by each situation.

(Thucydides 1.22)

Most ancient writing was written to be read aloud and therefore needed to be dramatic and entertaining; this style of historical writing is sometimes known as 'rhetorical'. So although we must assume that the speech is 'made up', it would have been written by Plutarch to represent the sort of things that Tiberius Gracchus might have said. It is also a useful vehicle for putting forward arguments and persuading his audience that right was on the side of Tiberius Gracchus and the poor. We do know that some Gracchan speeches were written down and excerpts were quoted by later writers, and it is possible that the excerpt included by Plutarch is in fact authentic. However, we need to remember that Plutarch wrote in Greek, so the speech has at least been translated. I would also rather err on the side of caution and assume that speeches such as this are – to some extent – invented.

It is interesting to note that after the violent death of Tiberius Gracchus and many of his supporters, the land commission was not disbanded and its work of redistributing the *ager publicus* continued. This has led to speculation about whether it was Tiberius Gracchus' methods rather than his policies which prompted his downfall. What seems to have happened is that Tiberius found that he could never hope for the senate's approval for his legislation, so he took his measure straight to the people's assembly, over the heads of the senate. But his opponents in the senate had a supporter among the ten tribunes named Octavius.

Exercise

Read Plutarch 'Tiberius Gracchus' 11–15 in Reading 3.15 (b) and Appian 1.14 in Reading 3.16 (a). Which of Tiberius' political actions – as distinct from his policies – might have been seen as trespassing on senatorial prerogatives? (The work you did on the functions and powers of the senate in Section 2.2 might be worth reviewing before you begin to answer this question.)

RB

Discussion

We began this exercise with Tiberius' first offence: he ignored precedent by not gaining the senate's approval for his legislation before presenting it to the assembly. He then had a fellow tribune, Octavius, deposed by a vote of the assembly for attempting to veto his reforms. The veto was an important element of the constitution, as no magistrate held power alone. It was considered an important safeguard that the veto was always paramount in any disagreement between colleagues. Probably Tiberius' greatest offence to the dignity of the senate concerned the death of Attalus III of Pergamum. When the senate was cut out of the political equation by Tiberius' tactics, they responded by denying him any funds whatsoever for his programme. This meant that there was no money to provide the new settlers with tools or seeds. When Attalus died and bequeathed his kingdom to the Roman people, Tiberius decided that he would introduce a bill to use the money from Asia to finance his programme. He thereby trod on several senatorial toes: first by once again politically sidelining the senate, but most importantly by completely undermining their traditional responsibility for foreign affairs. A proposal more guaranteed to alienate and at the same time unify them can hardly be imagined.

The final insult is to be found in the extract from Appian. Tiberius stood for a second consecutive term as plebeian tribune. We have already seen that for ordinary magistracies this was prohibited by law – the consulship, for example, could only be held for a second time after a ten-year gap. But the tribunate was not an ordinary magistracy and there does not appear to have been a specific legal impediment to standing in consecutive years. Yet doing so went against the *mos maiorum*, Rome's age-old traditions and customs. One might have legitimately asked what there was to stop Tiberius Gracchus being elected year after year and basically doing whatever he liked. He would become a Roman Pericles or, even worse, a tyrant or a king. Clearly this was a currently held fear. Plutarch mentions in the context of the death of Attalus III that 'Eudemus of Pergamum had chosen a diadem and a purple robe out of the royal treasures, and presented them to him in the expectation that he would soon become king of Rome' ('Tiberius Gracchus' 14 in Reading 3.15). I think that this was a legitimate fear, but you will have to decide for yourself whether the real cause of the opposition was merely self-interest on the part of those who stood to lose out by Tiberius' proposals.

It seems to have been Tiberius' decision to stand for a second consecutive term that prompted his opponents in the senate to take action against him. In the confusion of the election, wonderfully evoked by Appian in Reading 3.16 (b), a mob led by Cornelius Scipio Nasica led an attack on Tiberius and his supporters. Tiberius and 300 of his supporters were clubbed to death and their bodies thrown into the Tiber. This was a crucial moment in Roman history: for the first time since the foundation of the republic, violence was used to settle a political disagreement. It was such a turning point that many have pointed to it as the moment when the Roman revolution, which ended with Augustus' establishment of the principate, began.

Gaius Gracchus

But the saga of the Gracchi was not over. As mentioned above, the three-man land commission continued its work. Originally it was composed, as you probably noticed, of Tiberius, his father-in-law Appius Claudius and his brother Gaius. New members were recruited to replace men who died: the vacancy created by Tiberius' death, for example, was filled by a man called Publius Licinius Crassus. There are several inscriptions from different parts of Italy which provide epigraphic evidence for the land redistribution programme. Each gives the names of the three land commissioners. Here are two examples of such inscriptions. The first provides evidence that Crassus replaced Tiberius Gracchus.

> [Near St. Angelo in Formis, 131 BCE] Gaius Sempronius Gracchus son of Tiberius, Appius Claudius Pulcher son of Gaius, Publius Licinius Crassus son of Publius, Board of Three for adjudging and assigning lands.
>
> (*CIL*, vol.1, 2nd ed., no.640)

This second inscription informs us that in 123 BCE the land commission was still going strong and that Tiberius' younger brother Gaius was still a member.

> [Near ancient Aeclanum, 123 BCE] Marcus Fulvius Flaccus son of Marcus, Gaius Sempronius Gracchus son of Tiberius, Gaius Papirius Carbo son of Gaius, Board of Three for adjudging and assigning lands. Estate allowed to established occupier free of charge*.
>
> [*This last phrase is a conjecture.]
>
> (*CIL*, vol.1, 2nd ed., no.643)

You will recall that Gaius Gracchus was exactly ten years younger than his brother, so from what you have already learned about the Roman system it will come as no surprise that in 123 BCE, exactly ten years after Tiberius held the office, Gaius was elected to the tribunate. Interestingly, he was re-elected the following year, thereby holding the office for two consecutive years, and no one seems to have raised any objections. Gaius packed a lot of legislation into his tribunate. In many ways it was more resonant than his brother's, in that he devised a personal programme which predicted many of the problems which would eventually cause the republic's downfall.

Exercise

Read the entry on 'Gracchus, Gaius' in the *OCCC*. Make notes on his legislative programme. The entry divides them into six parts. Keep this structure, but don't just copy the entries out: write them in your own words. (Don't worry if you don't fully understand them at this stage. We shall try to find some more evidence a little later.)

Discussion

Your list may look something like this:

1 A law designed to provide citizens with wheat at subsidised prices.

2 (a) Laws to carry on with land redistribution.
   (b) Laws concerning the foundation of colonies.

3 (a) Laws connected with army service.
   (b) Laws to fund public building projects.

4 A law to have the taxes of Asia 'sold' by the censors.

5 A law concerned with trials for provincial maladministration, especially about the composition of juries for such trials.

6 A law that was something to do with the senate's allocation of provinces.

7 A law giving 'Latins' Roman citizenship.

This should roughly resemble what you have. (I hope that you included the law to extend the citizenship, which was not given a number in the *OCCC*.) You might also have divided up those pieces of legislation which seemed to you to be two laws. There is no detail here, just a basic idea of the laws he proposed. You may also have felt that these laws were not explained particularly clearly. To add flesh to these bones we will need to look at the ancient sources which the authors of the entry on Gaius Gracchus in the *OCCC* used to write their synopsis. (They do not tell us what these are, but luckily we are already familiar with the main sources.)

Gaius' legislative programme

Exercise

Read Plutarch's 'Gaius Gracchus' 5–6 and 8–9 in Reading 3.17. Note down any references to laws in the extract. Which laws in your list does this extract provide evidence for?

Discussion

I managed to find evidence for the following laws on my list: 1, 2 (a) and (b), 3 (a) and (b), 5 and 7. I hope that you did too. (If not, go back and read the extract again.) I also expect you found that you understood some of the laws better, because Plutarch gives us more detail. I found no evidence for laws about changing the way that provinces were allocated (6) or about tax collecting in Asia (4). So we need to look at some other ancient sources to see if we can get some evidence for these. Let's try Appian next.

Exercise

Read Appian Book 1.21–23 in Reading 3.18. Again, note which of the laws on our list Appian provides evidence for.

Discussion

I only managed to find evidence for the following laws on my list from Appian: 1, 2 (b), 3 (b), 5 and 7. So this second source is useful in that it corroborates Plutarch and also adds a little more detail, especially about Rome's Italian allies. Appian tells us that Gaius proposed to give 'Latin' rights to the allies and make the 'Latins' full citizens. To find out the significance of this, we need to explore the different types of Italian communities.

Exercise

Read the section entitled 'Rome and Italy' in Beard and Crawford, Chapter Six, 'Rome and the Outside World', pp.77–82. In terms of status, list the different types of community found in Italy. Despite these differences, in what ways was Italy homogeneous? How would you characterise the grievances which led to the outbreak of the social war in 91 BCE?

Discussion

Beard and Crawford describe 'a mosaic of different types of community'(1999, p.77). You may have felt it might better be described as 'a confused tangle of different statuses and rights'. The three primary distinctions were between Roman citizens, those with 'Latin' rights, and allies. Full Roman citizens had the right to vote and stand for magistracies; they possessed all legal rights and were eligible for subsidised grain. They were also immune from *tributum* or direct taxation after 167 BCE. Those with 'Latin' rights, shared many of the civil and legal rights of full citizens. They were liable for military service and could even vote in the assembly, assuming they could make their way to Rome. The third group, the allies or *socii*, were those peoples who had a treaty with Rome. They shared in none of the rights and benefits afforded to citizens and Latins, but were crucial to Rome's military success.

Despite this great diversity there were significant factors that united Italy. There was, of course, the network of roads that tied Italy together. There was a common currency: citizens, Latins and allies served in the same army, and before the mid second century BCE enjoyed some of the fruits of conquest. There was also considerable linkage between the Italian and Roman élite. Italian businessmen were not slow in exploiting Rome's new provinces, as the events in Asia show. It also seems certain that the Italian élite occupied *ager publicus* and were thus affected by the Gracchan programme. When Gaius stood for a third term as tribune and was defeated in the election, it would appear that he lost because of his policy to widen the citizenship. The citizens on whom he relied for support were not prepared to share the benefits of their citizen status, such as cheap grain. So opposed to extending the citizenship were Romans generally that it took what was effectively a civil war to finally extend the citizenship to most Italians.

The Italians became very frustrated with this state of affairs. In 91 BCE, a war began between Rome and some of her allies. We shall not look at the war in detail, but its causes are interesting. About 160 BCE, Rome stopped founding 'Latin' colonies. These had previously provided a route for allies to attain Latin status as they had been allowed to join such communities. So one important reward for their loyalty and sacrifice was withdrawn. The demands for manpower made on the allies was also increasing during the second century BCE and they had to pay taxes, unlike citizens after 167 BCE. This led to the Social War of 91–88 BCE, a lengthy and bitter struggle which

Rome only won by granting full citizenship to most allied communities (see Figure 3.16). After the war all the inhabitants of Italy up to the River Po had become Roman citizens. The census figures, for this period show a doubling of the number of citizens, to 910,000, though this census was not taken until 69 BCE. All this could have been avoided had Gaius' farsighted proposal been adopted in 122 BCE.

Figure 3.16   Silver denarius (reverse), *c.*90 BCE. British Museum, London, BMC18 PCR 125. © Copyright The Trustees of the British Museum. Issued by the Italian allies during the Social War, it shows the bull of Italy trampling on and goring the wolf of Rome. The Oscan inscription which was read from right to left translates as 'ITALIA'.

But Appian has still not helped us find any evidence for laws 4 and 6 on our list. As I am sure you are aware by now, this is a typical problem for the study of ancient history: our main texts, which are our fullest sources, cannot be relied on to give us all the details we would like. In order to find the evidence we need, we would have to research among some more obscure ancient sources. One slightly less well-known ancient historian who left an account of Gaius Gracchus' legislation is Diodorus Siculus. Like our other two main sources, he was Greek, this time from Sicily. He was born around 90 BCE and wrote during the second half of the first century BCE, and is an earlier source than Appian or Plutarch. He lived for most of his adult life in Rome, but doesn't seem to have had friends among élite Romans in the way that Polybius did. Some of his sources can be identified, such as Polybius, and his personal philosophy (he was a Stoic) can be detected in his writings. He wrote a single compendious work entitled *Library of History* which was intended to be a comprehensive history of the human race.

Exercise

Now read the extract from Diodorus Siculus' *Library of History* below.

1   How would you describe the tone of this source? Try to find a
     short and memorable quotation in this extract, one that sums up
     Diodorus' view of Gaius' reforms. (When you read ancient
     sources it is always worth seeking out a succinct phrase which
     you can use in your own work to back up an argument.)

2   Can you find evidence for laws concerning tax collection in Asia
     or the allocation of provinces?

     By his public advocacy of the suppression of aristocracy and the
     establishment of democracy, Gaius Gracchus was able to draw on
     the willing support of all classes. Indeed, they became not just
     willing supporters but virtually the prime movers in his bold
     plans. Each and every one of them, inspired by his own selfish
     hopes, was ready to face any risk to defend the laws which began
     to be introduced as if he were defending his own private
     advantage. By stripping the senators of their right to sit in
     judgement and appointing the knights to serve as judges, he
     made the inferior element in the state master over the superior;
     and, by shattering the harmony which had existed hitherto
     between Senate and knights, he exposed both of them to the
     pressures of the mob. He split the state in two, thus paving the
     way for personal supremacy. He squandered the public treasury
     on disgraceful and ill-judged expenditures and bribes, so ensuring
     that he became the focus of all eyes. By sacrificing the provinces
     to the reckless greed of the public contractors, he wrung from the
     subject-peoples a justified hatred for the dominion of Rome. By
     currying favour with the soldiery through laws to relax the
     strictness of the old discipline, he opened the gates to anarchy
     and mutiny. For a man who comes to lose respect for those set in
     authority over him comes to lose respect for the laws as well; and
     such patterns of behaviour breed fatal disorder and national
     destruction ...
     (Diodorus Siculus 34)

Discussion

1   You were probably struck by the general hostility of this source.
     Diodorus seems to blame the Gracchan reforms for all the
     problems which beset the republic. He mentions quite a few of
     the laws we have already discussed and roundly criticises them.

The general tenor of his criticisms is perhaps best summed-up in the phrase: 'he made the inferior element in the state master over the superior'. This is my favourite quotation in the excerpt, though you might have chosen another one: 'He split the state in two' or 'he opened the gates to anarchy and mutiny'.

2   This extract finally provides us with evidence for the changes introduced to the system of tax collection in the province of Asia. This is important and we ought to look at the background a little. Gaius needed money to fund his schemes, such as the grain subsidy, the road building programme and other public works, as well as the establishment of colonies. All these schemes cost money, and, like his brother, he looked to Asia to provide it. Asia had become a province in 129 BCE and was exceptionally rich. Gaius decided to change the way that tax was collected by auctioning off the right to collect the various taxes. Rich equestrians formed companies to buy the rights to collect taxes but they had to pay the money up-front. These men, called *publicani* (the 'publicans' of the New Testament) then had carte blanche to collect as much tax as they could, ensuring that they covered their costs and made substantial profits. There is some truth in Diodorus' claim that this new system created 'a justified hatred for the dominion of Rome'. This is perhaps shown by events that took place about 50 years later in 88 BCE when Mithridates VI, king of neighbouring Pontus, 'liberated' Asia and ordered the massacre of all the Romans and Italians in the province. The citizens of Asia were so desperate and their hatred of Rome so deep-rooted – mainly because of the activities of the *publicani* – that they slaughtered around 80,000 men, women and children in a single night. It is worth noting that no distinction was made between Romans and Italians. To the population of Asia they were all *Romaioi* and were all guilty of exploitation.

So there is an irony in Gaius' law concerning the tax-collecting regime in Asia. It ensured that provincials were bled dry in order to provide for his schemes to help the Roman poor. It also represents something of a change in approach toward the provinces in general. Previously, provincial cities had been looted, with valuables, works of art and thousands of slaves carted off to Rome; from now on they were to be kept alive and milked. There is a further link between this legislation and one of the other laws transferring the courts from the senatorial to the equestrian orders. Senatorial governors had a fairly bad track record of corruption and enriching themselves at the expense of their provinces. If accused of corruption, they would be tried by a jury of their fellow senators and would nearly always acquitted. Appian gives some examples of this kind of corruption at the beginning of Book 1.22 (Reading 3.18), which you should refer back to. There was a problem to be addressed here, and perhaps on one level removing these courts from the hands of the senate made sense. The problem was that under the new tax-collecting regime, the only check on the rapaciousness of the *publicani* were the provincial governors. But now with the equites controlling the courts they could bring a senatorial governor to 'their' court on trumped up charges in the knowledge that he would be found guilty by a jury of fellow equestrians.

Exercise

One of the most famous incidents of this kind was the prosecution of Publius Rutilius Rufus in 92 BCE. Use the internet to find out as much as you can about this case. Go to the course website. You will find some useful links under 'Course links Block 3'.

Discussion

You should have been able to find out that Rutilius had a successful career, reaching the consulship in 105 BCE. He had something of a reputation for uprightness and discipline. While legate to the governor of Asia in 94/3 BCE he tried to protect the provincials by reining in the *publicani*. On his return to Rome he was prosecuted for extortion and convicted by an equestrian jury. He was sent into exile and chose to go to Asia, where he was rapturously received by the people he was convicted of exploiting and became a citizen of Smyrna.

You may have noticed that we have still not found any evidence for law 6 from the *OCCC*, which involved the allocation of provinces. So we need to look at more ancient sources.

Cicero's view of the legislation

In this case, it is Cicero who provides us with crucial additional evidence. Cicero was roughly contemporary with Diodorus Siculus and was active in the first century BCE. He has always been seen as hugely important to the latter stages of the republican period, so it would be worth finding something out about him now.

Exercise

Read the first three pages of the entry for 'Cicero' in the *OCCC*, just to get a general sense of who he was, what he did and so on. (You may also find Essay Six in *Experiencing the Classical World* useful too, but you will be reading it in more detail later in the block.)

Discussion

You probably got a sense of Cicero's significance by the size of his entry. I expect you noted that he was born in 106 BCE, was not from Rome itself and was from an equestrian, rather than a senatorial family. He then embarked on a public career, initially with military service, followed by a succession of magistracies, which he held at the earliest age possible, culminating in the consulship in 63 BCE. The entry also mentions his work as an advocate and he was (and probably still is) considered the most brilliant barrister that Rome produced. He was also a prolific writer, leaving us a large corpus of letters, forensic and political speeches, and philosophical works.

Exercise

Read the following extracts from various works by Cicero. What new light do extracts (a) and (b) shed on the law involving subsidised corn? What do extracts (c) and (d) tell us?

(a) Gaius Gracchus introduced a corn law. The commons were delighted, it made generous provision for the means of subsistence without their having to work for it. The *boni* found it repugnant, because they thought the commons were being encouraged to give up hard work and take to idleness, and they could see that the treasury was being drained dry.
(Cicero, *Pro Sestio* 103)

(b) ... so too Gaius Gracchus. Although he had granted extravagant doles and poured out money from the treasury like water, he nevertheless spoke as if he were the watch-dog of the treasury. Why should I pay attention to words when the facts are in front of my eyes? The famous Lucius Piso Frugi had consistently opposed the corn law. But once the law had been ratified, for all that he was an ex-consul, he came along to collect his corn ration. Gracchus noticed Piso standing there in the crowd, and with the Roman people listening asked him how he could reconcile his applying for his corn ration with his opposition to the law which made it possible. 'I do not care for this fancy of yours, Gracchus, to divide my goods among every Tom, Dick and Harry', replied Piso; 'but, since that is what you are doing, I shall claim my share.' Does not the conduct of that worthy and wise statesman make it plain that Rome's public wealth was being squandered by Gracchus' law? Yet read Gracchus' speeches and you will declare him to be the jealous guardian of the public purse.

(Cicero, *Tusculan Disputations* 3.48)

(c) Gaius Gracchus, who was far and away the greatest of all popular politicians, not only did not take the allocation of the consular provinces away from the Senate, he even passed a law that required them to be decided annually by the Senate.

(Cicero, *De Domo* 24)

(d) The farmers who bought the Asian taxes from the censors complained in the Senate that they had been led by over-eagerness into making too high an offer and asked for the cancellation of their contract.

(Cicero, *Ad Atticum* 1.17.9)

Discussion

There was clearly a feeling that providing subsidised grain to citizens would make them lazy. In passage (a), Cicero mentions that a group called the *boni* were particularly opposed to it. The term translates as 'good men' and it was how conservative senators styled themselves. Another term often used to describe those who opposed the sort of reforms proposed by the Gracchi is *optimates*, with those like the Gracchi generally known as *populares* because they were seen to champion the 'popular' cause. It is important to note that these were not political parties in any modern sense – there were no parties in Roman political life. Alliances shifted; a group of senators might coalesce around a particular issue, only to break up once it had been supported or opposed. Passage (b) tells us that there was no means test for those citizens who could obtain subsidised grain, which is something we might have expected.

In passage (c) it is noteworthy that Cicero tells us that Gaius Gracchus (*not* Tiberius) was 'far and away the greatest of all popular politicians'. He also confirms the law involving the allocation of provinces. Let's consider what this law was all about. After a consul had completed his year of office, the senate decided which province he would govern. Some provinces were much more lucrative than others; it was thought that this process of allocation was susceptible to corruption and manipulation. Under this law the senate had to announce which provinces particular consuls would go on to govern at the time of their election, a full eighteen months before they took up their post.

With the death of Gaius Gracchus, it might have appeared that the conservative element in Roman politics, the *optimates*, had won, but in many ways it was a Pyrrhic victory. It is true that most of the Gracchan programme was rapidly dismantled. Colonies were annulled and the law to provide subsidised grain was moderated, perhaps by excluding freedmen. The allotments given to poor farmers, which had originally been inalienable, could now be sold, and the rich once again began to buy up small farms. Soon, further distributions were halted and the three-man land commission wound up.

But it was not really a victory at all: deep divisions within Roman society had been exposed. The Gracchan reforms had been ruthlessly and violently overturned, but the mood of the *boni* seems to have been one of apprehension rather victory. The Gracchi were not forgotten, either by the people or by those who sought power. Marius and Caesar, for example, both styled themselves *populares*, for they realised that the Gracchi had shown them a route to unprecedented personal power by using the people. Men such as these may not really have had the interests of the people at heart: espousing 'popular' causes may have simply been a means of attaining personal power. But the Gracchi had exposed real bitterness and deep-seated grievances, which their *populares* successors could stir up and play on whenever they felt the need.

4.2   Marius and Sulla

Marius

One might ask what would have happened if the Gracchi had had the support of an army. One of the first men to exploit the popular cause for personal ambition was Gaius Marius. Marius was a 'new man' (*novus homo*) in the sense that he reached the consulship although none of his ancestors had even been members of the senate. He was not from Rome but was born in Arpinum in 157 BCE to an equestrian family. Despite his comparatively humble origins, Marius embarked on the *cursus honorum*. He had the support of one of Rome's most aristocratic families, the Metelli, who dominated the consulship in the late second century BCE. Their patronage allowed him to reach the quaestorship in 123 BCE. This was followed by the tribunate in 119 and, amid allegations of bribery, he managed to be elected praetor in 115. After service as proconsul in Spain, he married a member of the patrician Julian family: Julius Caesar's aunt.

Marius' real opportunity for advancement came in a long war Rome fought against Jugurtha, King of Numidia. Numidia bordered the Roman province of Africa, and Jugurtha had come to power after a civil war during the course of which some Italian businessmen were killed. War was declared, but the first consul sent out in 112 BCE, Bestia, returned to Rome with a peace treaty which looked suspiciously favourable to Jugurtha. Amid allegations of bribery and corruption a tribune named Mamilius established a commission of inquiry to look into the affair and into aristocratic corruption generally. It is noteworthy that Opimius, the man responsible for the death of Gaius Gracchus, was brought before it and sent into exile along with Bestia and several other consulars. This shows us that the issues raised by the Gracchi were still very much alive and that the two brothers had not been forgotten. The next consul sent out to prosecute the war was another aristocrat, Spurius Albinus, who suffered defeat and humiliation at Jugurtha's hands (early 109 BCE). When, in the summer of 109 BCE, the consul Metellus was sent to Numidia, he chose Marius as his senior legate.

Exercise

Read Plutarch's 'Life of Marius' 7–8 in Reading 3.19. How did Marius seek to undermine Metellus? Why was Metellus' comment about when Marius should stand for the consulship such an insult?

Discussion

It would appear from this extract that Marius had a coherent plan to undermine Metellus, both in Africa and at Rome. Presumably its purpose was to increase his chances of being elected consul for 107 BCE.

Marius was a very talented soldier and was able to gain the respect and loyalty of the army, who wrote letters home to the effect that he was the only man capable of beating Jugurtha and should be elected consul. You might suspect that this letter-writing campaign was engineered by Marius to put pressure on Metellus. You might also have thought it relevant that in 107 BCE Marius would be fifty years old – already long past the earliest age (42 or 43) at which he could have held the consulship. Metellus' son was probably about twenty when Metellus made this comment, so he was almost telling Marius to give up any thoughts of higher office.

Sallust, in his account, confirms this incident and has Metellus say: 'do not entertain ambitions beyond your station. All things are not for all men to aspire to, you must rest content with what you have ...' (Sallust, *The Jugurthine War* 64).

Exercise

Sallust also confirms the notion that Marius was waging a well thought-out propaganda campaign against Metellus. Read the following extract. From which group or groups did Marius hope to get support for his bid for the consulship?

> By such means he won over ... a number of Roman Equites who were either serving in the army or engaged in trade, persuading them, partly by his personal influence and partly by raising their hopes of peace, to write to their friends in Rome severely criticizing Metellus's conduct of the war and demanding that Marius should be given the command. In this way he secured a large body of supporters who urged his claims to the consulship in the most complimentary terms; and just at that particular time the commons, taking advantage of the defeat inflicted on the nobles by the law of Mamilius, were doing all they could to get new men elected. Thus everything favoured Marius.
>
> (Sallust, *The Jugurthine War* 65)

Discussion

This source adds important additional information. It suggests that Marius was indeed conducting a co-ordinated campaign and it makes clear that the support of the equites was crucial. Marius was taking advantage of the 'popular' feelings aroused by the Mamilian commission. It also perhaps shows the extent to which internal politics were beginning to dominate foreign affairs.

Back in Rome, Marius proceeded to draw a distinction between himself – a simple man of the people – and the corrupt, lazy and incompetent aristocrats. Sallust puts a very long speech into his mouth which reveals how Marius sought to appeal to the 'people'. He was clearly seeking to exploit those divisions in Roman society revealed by the Gracchi.

Exercise

Read the extracts from Sallust, *The Jugurthine War* 85 and Plutarch, *Life of Marius* 9 in Readings 3.20 and 3.21.

1   What criticisms does 'Marius' make of the aristocracy?

2   Which points would you need to make about Sallust as a source
    if you intended to use it to illustrate a historical point?

3   Can you find a reference to something Marius did which appears
    to be a clear departure from traditional practice? (You might find
    p.7 of Beard and Crawford useful here.)

Discussion

1   Some of the criticisms are general and some specific. Generally,
    according to Sallust, aristocrats are indolent: they owe their
    advancement to their name rather than their talent. They are
    arrogant and cowardly, love luxury and behave like women. They
    are unworthy of their great ancestors (it's interesting to note the
    comparison that is drawn between the present generation and
    their ancestors). As commanders, they live in luxury while their
    men suffer and toil under their severe discipline. The generals
    who have so far led the army in Numidia have been vain, greedy
    and incompetent as well as corrupt, arrogant and rash.

2   Of course, we do have to be very careful in suggesting that
    Marius thought these things. Clearly we must assume that the
    speech is manufactured, and it seems to fit in to Sallust's own
    agenda which we discussed earlier in the block. But it seems to be
    supported by Plutarch, who confirms that Marius did indeed
    exploit divisions between the aristocracy and the people, and was
    critical of the conduct of the war by aristocratic commanders. We
    could also expect the speech to contain the sort of things that
    Marius *might* have said or even express sentiments that he was
    well known for, because Sallust was writing reasonably closely in
    time to the events. Plutarch also mentions 'violent speeches, full
    of contempt' (Gaius Marius 9), so perhaps you feel that we are on
    fairly safe ground in suggesting that Marius made inflammatory
    speeches, critical of the aristocracy.

3   I expect you managed to find, towards the end of the extract,
    Sallust's reference to Marius' recruitment of soldiers from the
    proletarii. Plutarch mentions it too, and it was a very important
    development, with important repercussions. Beard and Crawford
    make the point that this had been done before in times of great
    crisis (1985, p.7), but Marius did it openly, which was new. These
    new recruits were all volunteers: they would be paid, receive a
    share in any booty and a grant of land on completion of their
    terms of service. They looked to their generals to provide all

these benefits. They thus became bound in loyalty to their commanders rather than to the state, the senate or the people. Of course, under the Roman system, generals also had to be active politicians and have achieved high office. You can perhaps see what a potentially dangerous situation was created by an apparently small change in recruitment practice.

The career of Marius is littered with such precedents. After his election to the consulship in 107 BCE, the people, against the will of the senate, gave him the African command. While Marius was conducting the campaign against Jugurtha a new threat arose, this time just over the Alps in the province of Transalpine Gaul. Two huge Germanic tribes had been wandering around Gaul for about a decade. In 105 BCE they inflicted a huge and unprecedented defeat on two Roman armies at Arausio (Orange): the sources tell us that 80,000 Romans were killed in a single day. An alliance between the people and the equites clamoured for Marius' re-election as consul for 104 BCE, believing that only he could save Rome. So at the elections in the summer of 105 for the consulship of 104, Marius was elected even though he was still fighting in Numidia and had been consul only two years previously. As it turned out, the German tribes did not threaten Italy in 104 BCE, but Marius managed to defeat them in 102 and 101, when he was consul for the fifth time. His sixth consulship came in 100 BCE and he even held a seventh consulship in 86, which was entirely unprecedented. Clearly the ten-year rule had been seriously breached.

Marius achieved far greater power and *auctoritas* (which translates as 'authority' but had more resonance in a Roman context) than any aristocrat ever had. He was an excellent soldier and general, but as a politician he was not so successful. We have seen how he exploited 'popular' sentiment in order to gain his first consulship, but he never seemed really committed to the popular cause. His career ended at the age of 71 in a welter of bloody vengeance against those he perceived as his enemies. Plutarch, referring to the year 86 BCE, describes how:

> Marius's rage and thirst for blood increased from day to day as he kept on killing all against whom he had even the remotest grudge. Every road and every city was full of men pursuing and hunting down those trying to escape.
>
> (Plutarch, *Marius* 43)

Sulla

Marius' successor, Lucius Cornelius Sulla, was already waiting in the wings. Sulla had a quite different background from Marius.

Exercise

 Read the entry for 'Sulla' in the *OCCC*. In what ways did Sulla's background differ from that of Marius?

Discussion

In contrast to Marius' fairly humble origins, Sulla was from an old patrician family who had fallen on hard times and were completely impoverished by the time Sulla reached manhood. In fact, Sulla was only able to embark on a political career because he inherited wealth from his stepmother. Politically he was not a *popularis*: we have already noted his association with the Metelli, both politically and through marriage.

I won't go into too much detail on Sulla except to note how he took personal power a step further. He served under Marius in Africa and again against the German tribes, but their relationship was always uneasy. Sulla was elected to consulship for 88 and in 87 BCE was given the command against Mithridates. As we noted earlier, in 88 BCE Mithridates had ordered a massacre of all the Romans and Italians in the province of Asia and went on to occupy Greece. But just as Sulla was about to embark with his army for Greece, a tribune named Cinna passed a law giving the command to the 70-year-old Marius. Sulla turned his army round and marched on Rome forcing Marius to flee to Africa. Sulla then left for the east which allowed Marius to return to Rome. It was at this point then that Marius embarked on the terrible killing spree we have already mentioned. Sulla defeated Mithridates but made a settlement with him which left the king in control of Pontus before returning to Rome in 83 BCE.

While Sulla had been in the east, Rome had been under the control of men such as Cinna who supported his old (but now dead) enemy Marius. Sulla defeated their forces and took control of Rome. He then embarked on a bloody process of proscribing his enemies. This involved publishing lists of names of those who could be killed with impunity for a large financial reward. Many were political opponents, but some were killed simply for their property. Plutarch tells us about:

> Quintus Aurelius, a man who had nothing to do with politics and
> who imagined that he was only connected with these disastrous
> events in so far as he sympathized with others who were in
> distress. He went into the forum and, reading through the list of
> condemned, came upon his own name. 'Things are bad for me,'
> he said; 'I am being hunted down by my Alban estate.' And he
> had not gone far before he was cut down by someone who had in
> fact been hunting after him.
>
> (Plutarch, *Sulla* 31)

It is in this period, 83–79 BCE, when Sulla had been made permanent
dictator and had killed all his political enemies, that we see his political
philosophy. As dictator he introduced a complex series of constitutional and
legislative changes.

Exercise

Read Appian 1.100 in Reading 3.22 and list the changes to the
constitution which Appian tells us that Sulla introduced.

Discussion

Appian does not give us a comprehensive account of Sulla's
constitution but he mentions the main components. He made the
tribunate a dead-end; anyone who held it could hold no other office,
thus making it extremely unattractive to any ambitious politician. He
doubled the size of the senate from 300 (though it was well below this
figure after his proscriptions) to 600. He also reinstated the law which
demanded that magistracies be held in order and that the ten-year gap
between consulships was properly observed.

Exercise

Now work through the list you made above and write a sentence or
two explaining why you think a particular change was made.

Discussion

These are my ideas. From the Sullan constitution we can see what
many conservatives must have thought were the basic problems with
the constitution. Sulla thought that he could set the republic back on
the right path by his legislation. In a nutshell, he wanted to bolster the
power of the senate and remove power from the people. He clearly
identified radical tribunes as a problem; neuter them, he must have

thought, and there would be no future Gracchi to threaten the status quo. He increased the size of the senate by adding a number of equestrians to its ranks. This he hoped might make the senate stronger and also more representative of Rome's ruling class as a whole. We can assume that all the new senators chosen by Sulla would be his supporters and would have a vested interest in defending his constitutional changes. His insistence that the magistracies were to be held in order and the gap between consulships observed was presumably designed to prevent extraordinary commands and successive consulships such as those held by Marius. Sulla surprised everyone by retiring in 79 BCE. He clearly felt he had laid sufficiently firm foundations for a new revamped republic with the senate once again firmly in control.

Civil war

Both Marius and Sulla are significant because of the way they used their personal armies to pursue political and personal aims. Both resorted to the mass murder of Roman citizens to quell any opposition, or simply for revenge. Many of those killed were wealthy and prominent citizens, senators and equestrians. It was an example that others followed: civil war, proscriptions, murder, all became an established part of the political process. But it was not long after Sulla's death in 78 BCE that his constitutional changes began to be eroded.

 Ironically, two of the prime 'nibblers' were his young supporters, Pompey Magnus (or Pompey the Great) and Licinius Crassus. Pompey had supported Sulla from the time of his return from the east and had served in Africa and Sicily against the dictator's enemies. Crassus had made himself the richest man in Rome, largely by buying up the properties of the proscribed at knock-down prices. They were joint consuls in 70 BCE, despite the fact that Pompey was below the minimum age and had held no prior magistracies. During their year of office they restored the powers that had been stripped from the tribunes by Sulla. Our sources suggest that they did not particularly like one another, but were prepared to bury their differences for what they saw as personal advantage. Look at Plate 42 in the Illustrations Book for a portrait of Pompey the Great.

From 66 to 62 BCE Pompey campaigned in the east against Mithridates. After finally defeating him, Pompey annexed Syria for Rome and imposed a lasting settlement on Asia Minor. He returned to Rome in 62 BCE at the head of a hugely powerful and loyal army, but he did not follow Sulla and march on Rome as people feared he might. He simply disbanded his army and returned to Rome with just a few close friends.

Despite this the senate did not trust Pompey and, after his return to Rome, they tried to impede him at every turn. This eventually drove him into the arms of the up-and-coming politician Gaius Julius Caesar. In 59 BCE, frustrated by the senate's refusal to ratify his eastern settlement and provide land for his veterans, Pompey joined Caesar and Crassus in an informal pact of friendship known to modern historians as the First Triumvirate. This pact was cemented in the same year by the marriage of Pompey to Caesar's daughter Julia. Unlike many political marriages, this one seems to have been a love match; our ancient sources suggest that Pompey and Julia doted on one another.

But by 50 BCE Crassus had been killed in Parthia and Julia had died in childbirth. Pompey had transferred his allegiance to the senate and was now the defender of the republican constitution against his old ally and ex-father-in-law Caesar. In 49 BCE Caesar left his province of Cisalpine Gaul and crossed a small and insignificant river, named the Rubicon, which marked the boundary of Roman Italy.

Civil war between Pompey and Caesar ensued, from which Caesar emerged victorious. He made himself permanent dictator of Rome with a young man named Marcus Antonius as his deputy, or Master of Horse. To most of Rome's élite the position was intolerable and a plot was hatched to free Rome from the tyranny of Caesar. Thus it was that on the Ides of March 44 BCE Caesar was stabbed numerous times while attending a meeting of the senate being held in part of Pompey's theatre complex. The plotters thought naively that simply killing Caesar would bring about a restoration of the republic. They could not have been more wrong.

4.3   The forum: a theatre of power

In this short section you will work with DVD3, Section 4. It aims to consolidate your study in Block 3 up to this point by drawing out and illustrating the main points so far, and enables you to study more of the archaeology of Rome.

You have already seen how the Roman élite used the Campus Martius as a place to both vaunt and commemorate their achievements. But the stage on which much of the political action took place was the Roman forum. The Roman forum has undergone many changes in nearly three thousand years of use. We are going to concentrate on less than 200 of those years between about 200 and 1 BCE, and investigate in detail only the northern end of the forum. You have studied the political organisation of Rome and some episodes from its history: now you will study some of the archaeological remains of the places where that action took place.

Unfortunately for our purposes, the forum was completely remodelled by Julius Caesar and Augustus. Although when you visit the site of the *forum*

Romanum today you can still see the rostrum from which speakers addressed the assembled citizens and the *curia* or senate-house (where senators carried out their deliberations), the actual buildings are later replacements. So the challenge is to work back from what is there now to understand what it was like in the republic. At the same time it will be possible to consider some of the legendary associations of the place and study how the forum came to be a place for the commemoration of great deeds.

Exercise

Watch DVD3, Section 4, 'The Roman forum'. As you watch, tick off the topics you have studied so far in Block 3 on the list below when they are mentioned in the DVD.

Some topics are covered more than once and others not at all. The aim of this exercise is to encourage you to reflect on your study of the Roman republic so far, and to make connections between your study and the remains of the Roman forum.

Figures 3.17, 18 and 19 below provide plans of the area under consideration in the DVD.

> Greek colonies
>
> Poseidonia
>
> Etruscans and Greeks
>
> Greek culture and Rome
>
> The political system in the late republic
>
> The constitution of the Roman republic
>
> The problems of imperial success
>
> Building history: ancestors, achievements and children
>
> The tomb of the Scipios
>
> Public commemoration
>
> Genealogies
>
> Land, people and power
>
> The Gracchi brothers
>
> Marius and Sulla

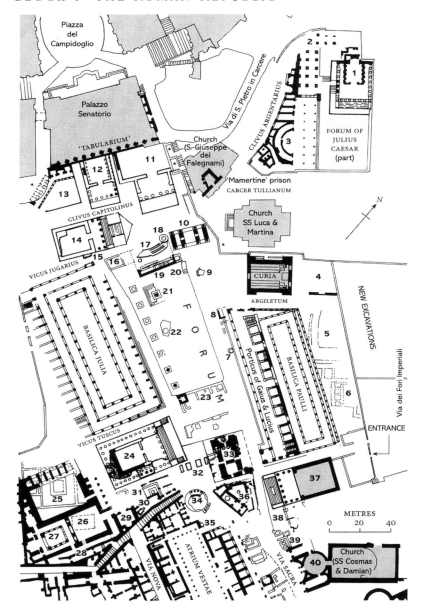

1 Temple of Venus Genetrix
2 'Basilica Argentaria'
3 Large public latrine
4 South corner of Forum of Caesar
5 South end of Forum of Nerva (part)
6 Part of Temple of Peace
7 Shrine of Venus Cloacina
8 Arch of Janus (?)
9 Black Stone (Niger Lapis)
10 Arch of Septimius Severus
11 Temple of Concordia Augusta
12 Temple of Vespasian and Titus
13 Precinct of the Harmonius Gods
14 Temple of Saturn

15 Arch of Tiberius (?)
16 Lacus Servilius (?)
17 Caesarian Rostra
18 Umbilicus Urbis
19 Augustan Rostra
20 Decennalia base
21 Column of Phocas
22 Lacus Curtius
23 Late Imperial Rostra
24 Temple of Castor
25 Domitianic Hall/*Domus Gai* (?)
26 Forecourt (S. Maria Antiqua)
27 Atrium (S. Maria Antiqua)

28 Covered ramp to Palatine
29 Oratory of the 40 Martyrs
30 Shrine of Juturna
31 Lacus Juturnae
32 Arch of Augustus
33 Temple of Divius Julius
34 Temple of Vesta
35 Shrine
36 Regia
37 Temple of Divus Antoninus and Diva Faustina
38 Archaic burials
39 Basement of a late republican house
40 'Temple of Divus Romulus'

Figure 3.17 Plan of the Roman forum in the late imperial period and surrounding modern buildings, from Amanda Claridge, *Rome: An Oxford Archaeological Guide*, Oxford University Press, 1998, p.60.

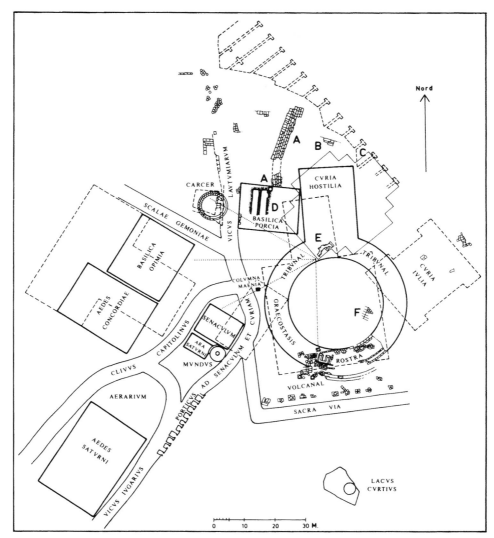

Figure 3.18   Plan of the republican *comitium* and neighbouring buildings, from Eva Margareta Steinby, *Lexicon Topographicum Urbis Romae*, Volume Primo, seconda edizione, Rome: Edizioni Quasar, 1993, fig. 182, credited to da Coarelli, *Foro Romano*, 1,139, fig. 39. Earlier and later buildings are shown with a dashed line. The Curia Iulia and the Aedes Saturni (Temple of Saturn) are the only well-preserved structures.

Discussion

The DVD concentrates on showing you the locations where political processes took place and relates the various locations to individuals associated with them, either through myth or through patronage. As in DVD3, Section 3 on the *Campus Martius*, the gods and their temples are a prominent element of the cityscape. One particular feature to

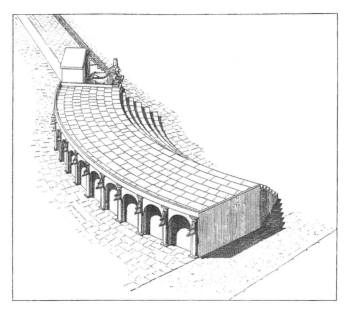

Figure 3.19   Reconstruction of the republican rostrum
viewed from the east, from Eva Margareta Steinby, *Lexicon
Topographicum Urbis Romae*, Volume Quarto, Rome: Edizioni
Quasar, 1999, fig 95, credited to: E. Gjerstad, *OpArch* 2.2
(1941), 143, fig. 1.0.

note is how the DVD refers back to the city of Paestum, which you
studied in the introduction to the block. In DVD3, Section 1 both the
political elements of Paestum and its buildings were discussed as being
influenced by the city of Rome. Now that you have studied the centre
of Rome it should be clearer to you how the colonies of Rome
reproduced some elements of the mother-city.

4.4   Organising historical evidence

So far in this part of Block 3 we have concentrated on gathering and
analysing evidence. I also hope that you will have gained some insights into
the process of historical research. Primary or ancient evidence provides the
crucial building blocks with which a historical account can be constructed.
But having sifted and assessed your evidence you need to decide how to
organise it. It is on this process that I wish to concentrate in the final part of
the block.

Exercise

Historians, both ancient and modern, organise their material in several different ways. It is something you have had to do as you have worked through A219. Imagine that you need to focus on a specific decade. Note down the different ways that you might organise a historical account of that particular decade.

Discussion

The most obvious structure would be a chronological or even an annalistic one. This is quite a common approach among Greek and Roman historians such as Thucydides and Tacitus. You probably also noted that a biographical approach is often used, one that concentrates on key figures. Plutarch does this and our bookshelves are full of modern biographies. Another approach would be thematic, where particular themes are explored. You might also have thought of concentrating on particularly important events within a period.

Exercise

Now consider the drawbacks to these different approaches.

Discussion

Before tackling this, it would be worth considering what you are trying to achieve. Good historical writing (yours and anyone else's) seeks to analyse the evidence and not just describe it. A rigid chronological structure might be a bit restrictive and encourage narration at the expense of analysis. What I mean is that it tempts you to use your evidence to tell a story of what happened rather than explain *why* it happened.

A biographical approach also has drawbacks. A focus on individuals may make them appear to be more significant than they really were. This approach might also mask wider cultural and political changes. Another problem in this particular subject area is that the only people about whom we really have enough evidence to adopt a biographical approach are élite males, which can easily distort our whole conception of the period. Beard and Crawford make some quite critical comments about biographical treatments and describe this approach as 'completely misguided' (1999, p.vii).

A thematic approach would appear to be the most fruitful and it certainly encourages analysis. However, when writing on historical subjects, you will need to discuss key figures and provide some sort of chronological framework. I would say that it is best not to be too prescriptive; some elements from all three methods might be required. The important point is to ensure that the different methods are used to analyse and explain rather than narrate or describe. As you work through the remainder of the block, be aware of which methods and techniques are being used.

4.5   Julius Caesar, Catullus and Cicero

In this section we will focus on three famous figures from the later Roman republic. In particular you will continue your work on historical methodology.

Exercise

Read Essay Six, 'Roman reputations: famous figures and false impressions in the late republic' in *Experiencing the Classical World*. (This will provide essential background to this part of the block.) As you read, consider ways in which the author, Paula James, arranges and organises her material and fill in the following grid. At this stage, simply note down which themes, people, events and dates are covered in reasonable depth, rather than merely mentioned. Then think about which elements are most prominent.

People	
Themes	

Events	
Dates/Chronology	

Discussion

My grid looks like this:

People	• Cicero • Catullus • Julius Caesar • Pompey • Publius Clodius • Clodia • the Gracchi
Themes	• the prominence of individuals • the equestrian order • literary sources as historical evidence (poetry, letters, forensic speeches, war commentaries) • the increasing power of generals • games • interpretations of modern scholarship
Events	• Caesar's campaigns in Gaul and his assassination • the death of Cicero's daughter, Tullia • the trial of Caelius

| Dates/Chronology | • There are not many dates. A general chronological sense of the period under discussion is given in the opening paragraph 'the first century BCE'. |
| | • The date of Caesar's assassination is also given as well as the date of Catullus' poem. |

This essay is a good example of the mixed approach that we discussed earlier. Themes are clearly important, but they are accessed and illustrated through people. This use of 'voices from the past' gives the discussions a human dimension and makes them more accessible and simply more interesting (an often underrated quality). The lack of too many dates is also quite interesting. It allows the writer freedom to roam within the established chronological framework without too much interruption. Where dates are given, such as the date of Catullus' poem, they have a very specific purpose and relevance. But the writer clearly doesn't feel obliged to provide them merely for their own sake. Like dates, events are used to give shape and context to the discussions. Of course, the one crucial 'event' that lingers in the background throughout the essay is the end of the republican system.

This would be a good point for you to listen to CD4, 'Poetic voices, political worlds', Tracks 1–25: the opening interview about reading and responding to Catullus. Kate Hammond is talking to Paula James about the poet and his place in Rome's 'high society.' Their discussion will give you further insights into the impact poetry could have upon personal lives and public careers in the late republic. Do bear in mind that our conclusions are necessarily tentative about Catullus' part in creating positive and negative spin around important political figures, and even somewhat speculative about reconstructing his turbulent affair with Lesbia. You will have gathered from reading Essay Six that we are dealing with a wealth of contemporary evidence but also a 'labyrinth' of attitudes and partisan perspectives. On the other hand, the interview gives a good demonstration of how we can progress through different levels of engagement with literary texts and frame questions about their form, function and historical significance. We can feel confident that we are finding out facts, not just gaining impressions.

Cicero and the Claudii
Up to this point in Block 3 a recurrent theme has been competition between members of the élite families of Rome, competition for power, prestige and reputation. It has been possible to study this in a wide variety

of sub-disciplines of Classical Studies: you've seen it in politics, tombs, literary culture, buildings and art. At the end of the Roman republic, written sources were particularly plentiful and detailed. As a result, it is sometimes possible to follow the ins and outs of politics on a daily basis by studying surviving letters written by those involved in the politics themselves. It is possible to go beyond the slightly abstract study of families, and how they competed, and look at cases where competition went far beyond rivalry to the point of animosity and personal abuse.

This subsection will investigate how rhetoric was used as a weapon in a clash between the newcomer Cicero, the first of his family to enter the senate, and one of the most successful of all the élite families, the Claudii. The latter's history of honours and achievements stretched right back to the very dawn of the Roman republic, when they achieved their first consulship in 495 BCE. Before the end of the republic, they had achieved dozens of consulships, many censorships and triumphs and numerous other magistracies. They remained prominent even after the republican system collapsed, lending their name to Rome's first imperial dynasty, the Julio-Claudians.

The particular generation of this patrician family that I wish to focus on was very active in the period up to 50 BCE. The most well-known member of the family is probably Publius Clodius Pulcher. Note that his family name is 'Clodius' rather than 'Claudius'. It appears that he preferred the plebian form of his name to the patrician form 'Claudius'. He was one of six children born to Appius Claudius Pulcher, consul in 79 BCE and a lieutenant of the dictator Sulla.

Publius Clodius had two brothers and three sisters. As the third and youngest son, his climb up the *cursus* would have been difficult. High achievement would have been expected of the young Clodius but, according to the generally hostile sources, his youth was notable for indiscretions rather than honours and achievements.

Exercise

Read the entry for Publius Clodius Pulcher in the *OCCC*.

- How would you characterise Clodius' politics?
- What was his relationship with Cicero?

Discussion

Clodius was clearly on the popular wing of Roman politics. Note how he was even prepared to be adopted by a plebeian in order to stand for the tribunate. There was a deep enmity between Clodius and Cicero. As tribune, Clodius introduced a law which resulted in

Cicero's exile in 58 BCE. He was recalled after about sixteen months and then, in 56 BCE, he saw a chance to have his revenge. Cicero embarked on the defence of a young aristocrat, Marcus Caelius Rufus, who was facing a variety of charges; two of the most serious were brought by Clodius' elder sister, Clodia, who was one of the republic's most famous women. As you have seen in Essay six, there is a strong possibility that she was the Lesbia of Catullus' poems. She was also the widow of a consul. Cicero's speech, an extract from which you are now about to read, brings us about as close as we can get to the drama of the proceedings.

Exercise

Read the extract from Cicero's defence of Caelius in Reading 3.23.

RB

1   How does this passage support the work you have done on the importance of ancestors?

2   As you read the passage, jot down any words which that you think describe Cicero's treatment of Clodia.

Discussion

1   The way in which Cicero uses Clodia's distinguished ancestors is fascinating. He actually assumes the character of Appius Claudius, who built one of Rome's first aqueducts as well as the eponymous Appian Way (Figure 3.20). Appius reminds his descendant of her worthy and distinguished ancestors, both male and female. This sense of being watched by one's ancestors, discussed earlier in the block, is very apparent. I hope that you also noted how Cicero mentions the importance of ancestral portraits.

Figure 3.20   Silver denarius of 56 BCE showing an equestrian statue of Q. Marcius Rex above the Aqua Marcia aqueduct. British Museum, London, BMC3891. © Copyright The Trustees of the British Museum.

2 I wanted you to give subjective responses to Cicero's treatment of Clodia. These were some of the words that occurred to me as I read the excerpt:

Cicero's treatment of Clodia is quite **cruel**, as she is not on trial after all. But Cicero puts her on trial in order to defend his client and insults her in the most scurrilous and spiteful way. However, some of his barbs are **amusing**, despite their cruelty. 'Was the sole purpose of my Road that you should parade up and down it escorted by a crowd of other women's husbands?' must surely have raised a few sniggers. It is very **hypocritical** that Cicero can defend Caelius' visits to prostitutes in an indulgent 'boys will be boys' way but condemn Clodia's indiscretions with such moral ferocity and indignation. Cicero's speech is very **theatrical**, especially in the way that he assumes other characters and generally paints such vivid and lurid pictures. Historically, of course, it affords an incredibly **interesting** glimpse into the lifestyle of Rome's *demi-monde*. Ultimately it was also **successful** as his client was acquitted.

Cicero is hugely important in any study of the death throes of the Roman republic. This is not so much because he was a particularly significant figure historically, but because he is a contemporary ancient source of unparalleled richness and depth. Cicero, of course, would probably disagree with this harsh, modern judgement, but he did tend to have an over-inflated opinion of his own historical importance. For example, he never let his contemporaries forget his consulship of 63 BCE and his suppression of the so-called conspiracy of Catiline.

It is primarily Cicero letters and speeches which give historians such an incredible and personal insight into the cataclysmic events of the mid first century BCE, especially those following the assassination of Julius Caesar on the Ides of March 44 BCE. Firstly, the glee that Cicero felt at the murder of Caesar is unconcealed. As he wrote to one of the assassins, Gaius Trebonius, almost one year later in February, 43: 'How I wish you had invited me to that superb banquet on the ides of March! Then we should have had no leavings' (*Ad Familiaris* 10.28). This last comment is a reference to Mark Antony, suggesting that Cicero felt that he should have been killed too. Antony was initially left in a very powerful position after Caesar's death and Cicero mounted a propaganda campaign against him. He delivered a series of scathing speeches denigrating Antony, with some very personal insults included, as this excerpt from his 'Second Philipic Against Antony', published in the autumn of 44 BCE, shows:

Then you graduated to man's clothing – or rather it was woman's as far as you were concerned. At first you were just a public prostitute, with a fixed price: quite a high one, too. But very soon Curio intervened and took you off the streets, promoting you, one might say, to wifely status, and making a sound, steady, married woman of you. No boy bought for sensual purposes was ever so completely in his master's power as you were in Curio's. On countless occasions his father threw you out of the house. He even stationed guards to keep you out! Nevertheless, helped by nocturnal darkness, urged on by sensuality, compelled by the promised fee – in, through the roof, you climbed.

(Cicero, 'Second Philipic Against Antony' 18, 1960)

Though purporting to be a speech to the senate, it was never actually delivered but instead distributed as a political pamphlet.

During the same period Cicero completely underestimated the youthful heir of Caesar, Octavian, who later became Augustus. In his letters, Cicero consistently refers to him as 'the boy' (*Ad Familiaris* 10.28). Cicero thought that he and the senate were manipulating Octavian for their own ends, in using him to crush Antony. However, Octavian was actually manipulating Cicero and the senate and, instead of destroying Antony, made a pact with him. This pact, know as the Triumvirate, also included a make-weight named Lepidus, and is usually known by historians as the Second Triumvirate to distinguish it from the informal pact between Julius Caesar, Pompey and Crassus formed in the 50s BCE.

These three men used their personally loyal armies to gain mastery of the state and embarked on their own series of proscriptions. The first name on their list was that of Cicero. In the process of attempting to escape by sea Cicero was intercepted by soldiers sent by the triumvirs. Plutarch describes what happened:

The officer took a few men with him and hurried round to the place where the path came out of the woods, and Herennius went running down the path. Cicero heard him coming and ordered his servants to set the litter down where they were. He himself, in that characteristic posture of his, with his chin resting on his left hand, looked steadfastly at his murderers. He was all covered in dust; his hair was long and disordered, and his face was pinched and wasted with his anxieties – so that most of those who stood by covered their faces while Herennius was killing him. His throat was cut as he stretched his neck out from the litter. He was in his sixty-fourth year. By Antony's orders Herennius cut off his head and his hands - the hands with which he had written the Philippics. (It was Cicero himself who called these speeches against Antony 'the Philippics'; and they have retained the title to the present day.)

(Plutarch, *Cicero* 48)

Antony ordered that Cicero's head and hands be mounted on the front of the rostrum in the forum, a symbolic fate for the great orator. Historians are constantly debating about when the Roman republic came to an end. The Battle of Actium in which Octavian defeated Antony in 31 BCE is often cited, but perhaps this moment deserves to be considered. It was more than just the death of a single statesman: it was arguably the death of the last republican.

References

Ancient sources

Cicero, *Pro Sestio* 103, *Tusculan Disputations* 3.48, *De Domo* 24 and *Ad Atticum* 1.17.9, in D.L. Stockton (trans.) (1981) *From the Gracchi to Sulla: Sources for Roman History 133–80 BC*, Harrow: London Association of Classical Teachers, pp.42, 43, 48.

Cicero, *Ad Familiaris* 10.28 and *Second Philipic Against Antony* 18, in M. Grant (trans.) *Cicero: Selected Works*, London: Penguin.

Diodorus Siculus, Library of History 34, in D.L. Stockton (trans.) (1981) *From the Gracchi to Sulla: Sources for Roman History 133–80 BC*, Harrow: London Association of Classical Teachers, pp.36–37.

Pliny the Elder, *Natural History* 34.31, in K. Jex-Blake (trans.) (1982) *The Elder Pliny's Chapters on the History of Art*, Chicago: Ares.

Plutarch, *'Lives' of Marius, Sulla and Cicero*, in R.Warner (trans.) (1958) *Fall of the Roman Republic*, London: Penguin.

Sallust, *The Jugurthine War* 64, in S.A. Handford (trans.) (1963) *The Jugurthine War/The Conspiracy of Catiline*, London: Penguin.

Thucydides, *The History of the Peloponnesian War* 1.22, in R. Warner (trans.) (1972) *Thucydides: The History of the Peloponnesian War*, London: Penguin.

Further reading

Modern scholarship

Brunt. P (1971) *Social Conflicts in the Roman Republic*, London: Chatto & Windus.

Flower, H. (ed.) (2004) *The Cambridge Companion to the Roman Republic*, Cambridge: Cambridge University Press.

Holland, T. (2003) *Rubicon*, London: Abacus.

Patterson, J.R. (2000) *Political Life in the City of Rome*, London: Bristol
Classical Press.

Sear, F. (1982) *Roman Architecture*, London: Batsford.

Tatum, W.J. (1999) *The Patrician Tribune*, California: University of North
Carolina Press.

Stockton, D. (1979) *The Gracchi*, Oxford: Oxford University Press.

Part 5 Poetry and cultural politics in Augustan Rome

5.1 Introduction

In the final part of this block we shall be taking a look at Augustus, Rome's first emperor, and considering the work of some of the major Latin poets who composed during this period. The study of Augustus will serve to consolidate your work on the breakdown of the Roman republican system earlier in the block and help you to see how this system was replaced and transformed – largely through the agency of one individual – into the imperial system that was to function as Rome's mode of government for the next few centuries. This system of government will serve as the backdrop to your studies of Roman social life in Block 4.

The establishment of the imperial system at Rome by Augustus also coincided with a phase of quite extraordinary artistic activity and achievement. In Part 3 of this block you considered the work of one of these great figures, the historian Livy. In this part of the block we will be taking a look at a group of literary artists working in a different medium: poetry. These authors – Horace, Ovid, Propertius and Virgil – are some of Rome's most famous literary figures. They worked at a time when political, social and artistic change and innovation all seethed away in the cultural boiling pot that was Rome at the turn of the first millennium CE. This intense social, political and cultural activity continued, and as the political situation stabilised, the scope for, and support of, artistic expression increased and flourished. Hence the Augustan period gives us a great opportunity to study and think about literature in its wider context and to reflect on the links between artistic products and the circumstances out of which they arise.

By the time you have worked through this material you should have a good knowledge of how Augustus came to establish the imperial system at Rome, the different types of poetry that were being produced in Augustan Rome, some of the fundamental issues of the age, and the way in which Augustan poetry was shaped by, and helped to shape, contemporary culture. You will also have thought about the issues surrounding the interpretation of poetry and the place of literature in society.

5.2 The Augustan principate

Augustus was the figure primarily responsible for the gradual transformation of the Roman republic into a new system of government: the system known as the principate. This 'imperial' Rome tends to be the ancient Rome that is most rooted in our consciousness: a state headed by an autocrat, the emperor (or more properly, princeps) who exercised supreme authority over his subjects across the broad geographical sweep of the Roman empire. This Hollywood image of a Rome ruled by a domineering monarchical figure is so familiar to us that it has a ring of inevitability and naturalness. However, as you have seen earlier in the block, from the time of the expulsion of the kings (traditionally 517 BCE) right down until Augustus' own day, Rome was actually a republic. This form of government was perhaps not particularly democratic and was heavily slanted towards the élite of Roman society but nevertheless there was a prescribed degree of popular participation for adult male citizens. This system was in effect the norm for Roman society for the best part of 500 years, though, as you have just seen, it was subjected to great strain and compromise at least from the time of the Gracchi. The transformation of Rome's form of government was perhaps inevitable given that the state had undergone such radical changes in its circumstances over the course of several centuries, but nevertheless we should not underestimate either the difficulty of the task or the ingrained sentiment for republicanism, particularly among Rome's ruling classes. These were men who were used to being leaders, not followers, who expected to participate actively in the government of the state; subservience and acquiescence were not generally part of their vocabulary. Rule by one man could be tolerated during the republic in exceptional circumstances for a limited period – but any attempt to consolidate such emergency powers into a constitutional position of supremacy ran a considerable risk, as Caesar found out on the Ides of March. The challenge for Augustus was to develop a system where he would be in a position to exercise ultimate authority while respecting (or appearing to respect) the sort of passionate feelings that led to the expulsion of the kings from Rome and the assassination of Caesar.

By now you will be quite adept at negotiating the entries in the *OCCC* and using these compressed accounts to help you both build up a general outline of the topic under consideration and also to answer more specific questions posed during the course.

Exercise

Read the *OCCC* entry on 'Augustus' and, drawing on your work from Parts 2 and 4 of this block and the introduction above, consider the following question:

- What do you think were the issues facing anyone trying to establish stable government at Rome during the period of the late republic?

Make some notes for yourself and reflect on what you have written before reading the following discussion.

Discussion

You might have thought here about the problems of bringing stability to a society that has gone through a protracted period of intense civil unrest. Once a clear-cut victor had emerged from the bloody chaos of the civil wars, what was the way forward that would avoid a relapse into the ruinous competition between ambitious strong-arm warlords? Was the old-style rule by the senate and people of Rome still viable? From your reading earlier in the block on the Gracchi, Marius and Sulla, you have seen the sort of fundamental divisions that existed in the Roman state and how difficult it was to reconcile conflicting interests without an eruption of bloodshed. Was the Roman republic a sufficiently robust system to stand up to a Roman general intent on imposing his agenda at the head of an army? Was there a way that the loyalty of Rome's troops to the state rather than to an individual could be ensured? One might also consider that Roman self-confidence and self-esteem needed to be re-established and that some sort of sense had to be made out of the chaos of the late republic. What had happened to Rome and why? These were some of the major challenges facing whoever arose as the victor from the ashes of Rome's civil wars in the late first century BCE.

Becoming Rome's first emperor

The person who arose as the phoenix from the ashes was Gaius Octavius, Julius Caesar's great-nephew. You will have read in the *OCCC* entry a brief account of how this young man, named as Caesar's heir, seized control of the Roman world in the bloody aftermath of Caesar's assassination. The process took over ten years before Octavius emerged as the undisputed master of Rome and its empire following his defeat of Mark Antony and Cleopatra at the battle of Actium in 31 BCE. Getting to the top, of course, was only half the challenge; now Octavius had the problem of how to stay there. Gradually Octavius shifted the terms under which he exercised his power and built up a new image of himself in which his pre-eminent position accorded with republican precedent and sentiment.

Figure 3.21   Cameo: Octavian in triumphant, heroic, nude pose. Intaglio with Augustus as Neptune, Roman, Imperial, Augustan Period, 31–27 BCE. Findspot: said to be from Tunis, Hadrumetum, Sard, length 2.1cm. Museum of Fine Arts, Boston. Francis Bartlett Donation of 1912, 27.733. Photograph © 2005 Museum of Fine Arts, Boston.

One thing Octavius did was change his name. In 27 BCE the senate voted him the new title of 'Augustus' (which roughly translates to 'revered'); this change of name was accompanied by a change in the way Augustus was depicted in public works of art. You can see from Figures 3.21 and 3.22 that the image of Octavius from before 31 BCE is quite different from that of the later image of Augustus. Augustus also promoted himself in the role of saving and restoring the Roman state; one of the honours that the senate granted him in 27 BCE was the right to have a *corona civica* (an oak wreath) fixed over the doorway of his house, an honour traditionally awarded to a Roman who saved the life of another Roman citizen. This symbol was adopted on Augustus' coinage and appeared along with the legend *ob cives servatos*, or 'for citizens saved' (see Figure 3.23). In similar fashion, a coin from 12 BCE shows a female personification of the Roman republic (denoted by the legend 'RES PUB') being raised from her knees by Augustus (Figure 3.24).

Figure 3.22   Statue of Augustus in the pose of a priest, *togatus capite velato* (in a toga with a veiled head). Marble, found in the Via Labicana, Rome, after 12 BCE, height 217cm, Museo Nazionale, Rome. Photo: Alinari Archives.

Figure 3.23   Gold coin (reverse), *c.*18–17 BCE, with a *corona civica* enclosing the legend *ob civis servatos* ('for citizens saved'). The British Museum, London (BMC314). © Copyright The Trustees of The British Museum.

Figure 3.24   Gold coin of 12 BCE depicting Augustus helping the fallen Roman republic to its feet. Taken from Paul Zanker, *The Power of Images in the Age of Augustus* (Ann Arbor: The University of Michigan Press, 1989). © The University of Michigan Press.

Augustus took active steps to make sure that it did not appear that he was monopolising Rome's highest magistracies and that the power he did exercise was vested in republican terminology. Hence, after 23 BCE, Augustus stopped holding the consulship every year; he maintained control over the provinces that contained most of Rome's troops through a grant from the senate of *imperium proconsulare maius*. *Imperium proconsulare* was the authority granted to an ex-consul as a governor of a province; by adding the qualifier *maius* ('greater') it ensured that Augustus had the final say in all of Rome's provinces. He was therefore granted all the powers of a tribune of the people and he actively refused titles that drew attention to singular authority such as dictator and sole consul. Thus, in the *Res Gestae* (literally meaning 'things done'), the account of his own life that he left behind to be inscribed on bronze pillars outside his mausoleum at Rome, and which also appeared as a monumental inscription elsewhere in the empire, he noted that he 'transferred the republic back from my power into the authority of the senate and people of Rome' and that 'after this time [27 BCE] I surpassed all in status yet I held no more power than those who were my colleagues in office' (*Res Gestae* 34). The title Augustus chose as the emblem of his position in the state was not emperor but princeps: the princeps *senatus* was the traditional title at Rome for the senior member of the senate. The basis of his authority was thus promoted as not one imposed from above but rather one exercised as a valued member from within a body of peers expressed by the Latin phrase *primus inter pares* ('first among equals'). Finally, in 2 BCE Augustus received by unanimous consent of the Roman community the title of *pater patriae* ('father of the state'); this title too was not without precedent as Cicero and Julius Caesar had both held it before him. The conferment of this title marks the culmination of the *Res Gestae*.

Exercise

Consider the account you have just read of how Octavius became Rome's first emperor and then reread the *OCCC* entry on 'Augustus'. You might also want to look back at your work on the Roman constitution and the different magistracies in Rome in Part 2 of this block.

Make some notes on what seems to you to be relevant material to help you answer the following question:

- Do you think Octavius really intended to restore the Roman republic or was he paying lip-service to the old constitution as a means of trying to avoid the fate of Julius Caesar?

Discussion

If you are like me you will have thought that avoiding aristocrats bearing daggers (the fate of Julius Caesar) must have been very much on the mind of Octavius after Actium. How could he convince Rome's aristocracy, who jealously guarded their right to participate in government, that normal service was being resumed? This was not an easy problem; to relinquish power can be as dangerous as to exercise it.

Certainly Octavius went through the motions of restoring the republic. As you have seen above, he formally declared in the *Res Gestae* that in 27 BCE he transferred control of the Roman state back to the senate and people of Rome, and that after this time his own authority was only ever on a par with his colleagues in office. Along the same lines, he actively promoted an image of himself as the saviour of the whole Roman state through associating himself visually with the emotionally charged emblem of the *corona civica* and by depicting himself on coins in a pose of helping a personification of the Roman republic to its feet (see Figure 3.24 above). All of this sent out a very powerful visual message of Octavius as the person responsible for personally resuscitating the Roman state and its subjects.

At the same time, it seems clear that Octavius was trying to put his old image behind him. Octavius' past was too obviously one of ruthless ambition, his ascent to power was bloody and the name of Caesar which had helped him on the way up was perhaps more of a liability than an asset once he got to the top. Caesar's legacy was, after all, one of trying to impose autocracy and of a violent and ultimately unsuccessful confrontation with Rome's aristocracy - not a particularly helpful image in the circumstances. So the ruthless young dynast formally known as Octavius (and more often than not just 'Caesar') became the more overtly benevolent figure of Augustus. You have seen in Figures 3.21 and 3.22 the sharp contrast between the swaggering, heroic, semi-nude figure of a triumphing Octavius and the figure of Augustus draped in a toga in a pose of reverential devotion.

Augustus also took pains to ensure that his own fairly radical position in the Roman state was enveloped in the trappings of tradition. Rome had no written constitution: what it relied on instead – as you saw in Part 2 of this block – was precedent and tradition. These principles came together under the Latin heading of *mos maiorum* (ancestral custom). Octavius had to convince Rome that his pre-eminence was simply an extension of tradition, and a natural outgrowth of the republican system and the sentiments on which it was based. Thus Augustus emphatically rejected anything that smacked overtly of autocracy: he would not consider titles such as 'sole consul', 'dictator' or 'king'; he stopped monopolising the consulship year after year. His adoption of the title of princeps and his espousal of the principle of *primus inter pares* all served to suggest an overt desire to lead from within, rather than from outside the parameters of republican precedent. This impression was bolstered by the fact that the executive authority he did exercise, such as the *imperium proconsulare maius* and tribunician power, were all apparently grounded soundly in republican institutions.

It might, then, seem as though Augustus had a genuine desire to restore the old system in Rome and only wished to act as the overseer for the duration of this process. But there is certainly a more cynical way of looking at all this, as implied in the question we are discussing. If we look at things from a perspective that suspects Octavius of putting his own interests before those of Rome, then we might see his behaviour as a complex process of misdirection and sleight of hand. The promotion of the image of him as the saviour of Rome was to cover up his own bloody role in the Roman civil wars – and the change of name and image that accompanied his transformation into Augustus was similarly designed to distance the present from the past. He merely paid lip-service to the republican ideals of shared executive power and limited tenure of office. The masking of his exceptional powers in traditional terms was nothing more than a sham that attempted to cover up his hoarding of executive power. For the powers associated with a variety of republican offices to be vested in a single person was not at all in keeping with the strict principles of Roman republicanism. It was all very well to resign the consulship, but he always received more back than he gave away. There was no hiding the fact of his pre-eminence and his pretence of being a *primus inter pares* was a conveniently chummy misrepresentation of the actual authority he possessed.

All of this could be seen as a carefully executed strategy to retain ultimate power while not wishing to run the risk of appearing to rub the noses of Rome's aristocracy in it. From this perspective, his professions in the *Res Gestae* of having restored power to the senate and people of Rome, and of exercising no more authority than his colleagues in office, were nothing more than empty political spin. If Augustus had wished to truly restore the republic, why hadn't he cut himself loose from his power bases? Why did he retain his executive authority for decade after decade?

The title of *pater patriae* was indeed an appropriate one for Augustus as it hinted at a sort of ingrained paternalism that Augustus appeared to embrace. The traditional powers of the Roman father (the *paterfamilias*) over the family unit were pronounced in Rome – you will read more about this in Block 4. The award of this title to Augustus suggests recognition of his similar ascendancy over the wider social unit of the Roman state. Augustus naturally would have liked to have thought of this as a form of benevolent and watchful paternalism, but a darker reading would see it as a form of overbearing authoritarianism.

That there were very different ways of viewing Octavius' ascent to power and Augustus' continued exercise of it is already apparent in the Romans' own thoughts about the matter. Tacitus, in his *Annales* (a historiographical work on Rome's early emperors composed around a century after the Augustan period), stages a mini-debate in Rome on the death of Augustus. The picture Tacitus presents is one of divided opinion, with praise and criticism being variously offered. Some saw autocratic rule as the only possible solution to the turmoil of the period of civil wars: the principate was not a dictatorship; law was re-established; force was only applied as necessary for the greater good of the majority. Others saw in Augustus an example of ruthless personal ambition, a man who let nothing stand in his way and who put his own desire for supreme power before the greater good of the state; peace was established but it was a *pax cruenta* (a bloody peace).

Trying to accurately assess a person's motivations 2,000 years after the event is an impossible task. The answer to the question of whether Octavius/Augustus was a ruthless self-serving opportunist or a self-effacing saviour of the Roman state is not straightforward (just as a lot of questions you have asked during the course are not straightforward). We might, for instance, question whether the terms within which this question is framed are useful, or if they give two options that are both too extreme; perhaps, as often, the truth lies somewhere in between such polar opposites. The Romans themselves weren't sure and neither can we be, but that shouldn't stop us from weighing the available evidence and drawing plausible conclusions based on it. At the same time, we must keep in mind that our own responses are inevitably, to some extent, informed by our own political and social values, even if we try our hardest to be objective, and that these values are also going to be a factor in arriving at our conclusions. The sort of questions that we need to ask to reach our own opinion of Augustus, such as how does one balance the need for security and law and order against civil liberty and democracy, are ones that we might also ask of our own world too.

Augustan Rome

In this subsection we move on to consider some of the principal policies of Augustus' principate, and in particular his legislation on marriage and adultery. Augustus wanted to preside over a Rome that would recover its traditional values, the sort of moral rectitude and downright decency that Romans liked to think had made their city the master of the Mediterranean in the first place. To this end, Augustus laid great emphasis on policies and ways of behaviour that he deemed in keeping with the ancestral spirit of Rome and its true values. In the *Res Gestae* he summed up this philosophy with regard to his own legislative programme and personal habits in the following manner:

> By bringing forward new legislation I recalled many ancestral habits
> that were disappearing from our own way of life and I myself handed
> down many exemplary habits to be imitated by posterity.
>
> (Augustus, *Res Gestae* 8)

This type of restorative and exemplary politics took many forms. For
instance, with regard to religion, Augustus embarked on a major
restoration of Rome's temples, noting in the *Res Gestae* that he repaired 82
temples in 28 BCE and neglected none that needed attention. Augustus
personally became a member of all Rome's priesthoods and the holder of
Rome's highest priestly office, the *pontifex maximus*, when its incumbent died
in 12 BCE. He revived and promoted various arcane traditions and offices.

At the same time as reviving past ritual and practice, Augustus also
attempted an ambitious programme of what we might call 'lifestyle reform'.
He wore clothes made by the female members of his own household; he
had his own daughter and granddaughters trained in spinning and
weaving; he taught his own grandchildren (who became his adoptive sons);
he tried to enforce traditional dress habits; he decorated his own house
simply and slept in the same bedroom for 40 years. Alongside this
promotion of himself and his family as paradigms, he also set about
legislating what did and did not constitute acceptable behaviour in certain
areas: extravagance, adultery, marriage and the manumission of slaves.

Marriage and adultery

We will concentrate particularly on the Augustan legislation in the areas of
marriage and adultery (this will provide important context for the studies of
Roman poetry that follow this section). In 18 BCE, Augustus put forward
two pieces of legislation dealing with adultery and marriage, the *Lex Julia de
adulteriis coercendis* (the Julian law about restraining adultery) and the *Lex Julia
de maritandis ordinibus* (the Julian law about marriage). This legislation
specifically targeted the Roman élite; its aims were to curb extra-marital
relationships and to promote marriage and re-marriage within this segment
of society in particular.

The legislation on adultery made this activity – for the first time in
Rome – a public criminal offence that was dealt with by a permanent court
(prior to this it had been a matter dealt with within the family). It should be
noted that adultery was defined as sex outside marriage between a Roman
citizen male and a married Roman citizen female, or between a married
female Roman citizen and any male. In other words, there was a
pronounced sexual double-standard here; a married male élite citizen could
legitimately have sex with slaves, ex-slaves and unmarried female members
of the citizen body of Rome's lower social orders, whereas a married female
élite citizen was expected to have sex only with her husband. Among the
terms of this law it was enacted that a woman convicted of adultery was to

be punished by confiscation of half of her dowry and a third of her property, and she was to be banished to an island. A man convicted of adultery was similarly to be punished by the confiscation of half of his property and also banished to an island – although obviously not the same one. The law also punished a husband who took no action on learning of his wife's adultery, as though he were a pimp – in other words, a husband had no choice but to divorce his wife if he knew of her adultery unless he wanted to be prosecuted himself. Fathers and husbands were given limited immunity for killing those discovered in the act of adultery.

The Augustan laws on marriage were designed to increase marriage and re-marriage among Rome's élite and provide incentives for the production of legitimate offspring. Restrictions were placed on matches that greatly transgressed the boundaries of Rome's social classes; for example, senators and their descendants were forbidden to marry ex-slaves or those who had themselves (or whose parents) been actors. Similarly, freeborn Romans in general were forbidden to marry prostitutes or ex-prostitutes, pimps or procurers, women convicted of adultery, or those who had acted on the stage. At the same time as certain restrictions were put in place on who could marry whom, the imperative to marry (and re-marry) was enforced. Marriage was effectively made mandatory for all men between the ages of 25–60 and women between the ages of 20 and 50. After the death of a partner, a woman was allowed one year before she was supposed to re-marry, six months if she had divorced (this was later increased in subsequent legislation in CE 9 to two years for a widow and eighteen months for a divorcee).

Incentives and penalties were also introduced for the production (or not) of legitimate children. Those who were childless (like those who remained unmarried) found their ability to inherit and leave inheritances curtailed. They could receive legacies and leave inheritances only to blood relatives; otherwise the state automatically became the beneficiary. Marriage with children was effectively legislated as a fast-track entry on to the career path, as those who fell into this category were given both precedence and the right to hold magistracies at younger ages. These child-related incentives were codified under the *ius trium liberorum* (the right of three children); marriage and the production of children also gave one the right to inherit and leave inheritances outside the family circle.

Exercise

Make some notes on the outline you have just read and refer again to the *OCCC* entry on 'Augustus' for additional information. Then focus on the following questions:

- How would you characterise the policies and general ethos that Augustus was promoting?

- Why do you think he was pursuing such a programme?

Discussion

While reading through the sort of policies and general mindset that Augustus promoted during his principate, words such as 'conservative' and 'reactionary' have probably sprung to mind. Augustus' policies were all about restoring what he saw as traditional Roman virtues and behaviour, such as piety, thrift and family.

When we speculate about Augustus' motivation, there are several possibilities. It might well have occurred to you that such a social programme was a natural postscript to his own attempt to integrate his position into the republican state apparatus. Thus Augustus' emphasis on traditional values and behaviour could be seen as part of his attempt to mask his own radical position in an aura of traditional conservatism. It is, of course, also possible that even if this *was* part of a deliberate strategy of manipulation, such policies were still a true reflection of his character and beliefs.

Along the same lines, we can see Augustus' social policy as a continuation of his image as the saviour of Rome. After the continued chaos and bloodshed of the late republican period, any new beginning had to be accompanied by a rejection of the immediate past and a new direction that would safeguard Rome in the future. In this manner, Augustus' social policies were promoted as a rejection of what was seen as the decadent and deficient behaviour that had left Rome in crisis. Thus, in the area of religion, Augustus' restoration of the temples, his revival of priestly offices and religious rites, and his membership of Rome's priesthoods, could all be viewed as a much-needed tonic to the religious neglect of the late republican period. Roman religion worked partly on a principle of maintaining the *pax deorum* (peace of the gods): neglect of religious duty had consequences: perhaps the failure of the Romans to honour their gods was behind all the suffering they had undergone during the civil wars. Augustus' gestures of piety could be viewed as putting this situation right and safeguarding Rome's future.

The same sort of justification could be used in terms of Augustus' 'lifestyle' legislation. His attempt to enforce certain standards sexual behaviour could again be viewed as a necessary corrective to the sort of immoral decadence in the late republic that had led to the collapse of the state. Once more, Augustus was just providing the cure that Rome needed in order to straighten itself out. The way forward according to this model was (rather paradoxically) to go backwards. You could even say that 'back to the future' was a cornerstone of Augustan social policy.

At the same time, though, that Augustus was overtly promoting a return to tradition, his own intervention through legislation into the lives of Rome's citizens was fairly radical. The Roman state was rather minimalist in the way it actively intervened in the everyday life of its citizens. Matters that affected the family and how its members lived their lives were largely matters for self-regulation. The Augustan legislation, however, represented an unprecedented (and sustained) state intrusion into the private lives of its citizens. This was not simply a matter of promoting certain types of behaviour and lifestyle but also an attempt to legislate morality: an intrusion, one might say, into every Roman's bedroom. In this manner, a general principle of self-regulation carried out within family units was replaced by a notion of *state* regulation: a 'nanny-state' philosophy, as we might say today. This form of intrusion was, of course, in keeping with Augustus' increasing paternalism, that culminated in his acceptance of the title of *pater patriae* in 2 BCE. As we noted earlier, he had in effect become the father of every Roman and was resolved to enforce the modes of behaviour and lifestyle that he saw fit on his family. When family and state blended in this way, then nothing was potentially beyond the regulation of state legislation.

In assessing Augustus' motivation, then, in pursuing these sorts of social policies, we run into the same sort of problems as we did when thinking about his rise to power. Were his policies a continuation of a deliberately manipulative strategy to cover over his own radical position with the trapping of traditional republican conservatism, or were they a heartfelt response to a crisis in the Roman state? Again the answer may lie somewhere in between, and our own response to 'conservatism' and 'tradition' will almost inevitably colour our judgement.

5.3   Horace's lyric poetry

Poetry in the Augustan age

By this point in the course you have studied a variety of different types of literature, from the epic of Homer to the history of Livy, works that span some 800 years or so of Greco-Roman history. You will be familiar by now with the course team's philosophy on how works of literature are intrinsically shaped by the historical circumstances and cultures in which they were produced. The context behind a piece of literature inevitably leaves its mark, but this is far from saying that there is no scope for individual expression. Within any society, people can potentially hold very different values, and the interaction between any single person and the society in which he or she lives is complex and unique to a greater or a lesser degree. If this was not the case, then every epic, tragedy and lyric poem written by anyone at any time would look the same. The point is not that the historical and cultural context of a piece of literature removes the possibility of individuality, but rather that such context is the framework within which authors work. How authors respond to this context can help us build up a picture, not only of the writer and his work, but also of the wider culture forming the backdrop to the writing process. The more authors we have from the same time, the better our chances of building up a coherent and illuminating picture of the period in question.

In the following sections we move on from Augustus to study some of the poetry produced during the time that he was in control of the Roman state. In the preceding sections of this part, we have studied and considered how Octavius/Augustus came to power and the sort of policies he instituted. The following sections focus on some of the famous literary figures of the Augustan period, both as a general introduction to the different types of poetry that they wrote, but also, through the use of case studies, as an examination of how their poetry interacted with the issues of the day. Your work here will thus be framed by the same concerns that have accompanied the study of literature throughout the course. Literary works are not just linguistic puzzles to be unravelled, but also important pieces of information on the culture within which their authors lived. Thus in Block 1 you studied Homer's *Odyssey* and *Iliad* as exemplars of epic poetry and also as sources (albeit ones that are very difficult to assess) for 'Dark Age' Greece. Similarly in Block 2, the study of Aeschylus' *Persians*, Thucydides' Funeral Speech and Aristophanes' *Lysistrata* not only gave you a chance to study the conventions of Athenian drama, historiography and rhetoric, but also to set these studies in the context of fifth century BCE history and society. Thus literature can be read and appreciated both in terms of the aesthetic pleasure it provides – and how it provides that pleasure – but also with a view to understanding what a work tells us about the cultural backdrop to its composition. In the same fashion, the following studies of Augustan poetry will aim to illuminate not just the mechanics and conventions of the different types of poetry that were being written at this time, but also how such literature serves both as evidence for a culture and an interpretation of it.

Lyric poetry

Our first subsection on poetry in the Augustan age deals with lyric poetry, in particular that of Horace. If you have the time, you might wish to do the following optional reading here:

- *OCCC* entry on 'lyric poetry' ('Latin' section)
- *OCCC* entry on 'Horace' (in particular, the introduction and the section on 'Odes (Carmina)')

Lyric poetry is a form of verse that goes back at least to the seventh century BCE and was originally performed to musical accompaniment on the lyre. In the ancient Greek world, lyric poetry could be performed either by a chorus or by an individual; in either case it was a spectacle forming part of a social occasion. We will concentrate here on solo lyric verse, or monody. Monody was typically based on less complex metrical patterns than choral lyric and it had a great variety of potential subject matter: love, war, friendship, mortality, drinking, praise, invective (abuse). The ancient Greek lyricists wrote in a variety of dialects and poetic metres and the canonical figures of Greek monody (such as Sappho, Alcaeus, Anacreon and Archilochus) flourished in the Archaic and early Classical periods of Greece. (You will have come across Sappho and Alcaeus already in the final section of Essay Three, 'Sing Muse: authorial voices in early Greek poetry' in *Experiencing the Classical World*.)

This then was a Greek form of poetry in origin, but like so much that was Greek it also found its way into Roman culture. When this type of verse was imported into Rome, what defined it in its Greek context inevitably changed. The specific social setting of Greek lyric poetry had disappeared into history and musical accompaniment was no longer a necessary or typical component. It is a generalisation, and one that is open to dispute, but we might say that lyric was transported from a performative context into a literary one; this isn't to say that lyric poetry was not performed in Rome, but that this social aspect of the poetry was increasingly subsumed by its wider circulation in written form. What did remain the same were the metrical patterns.

Horace

Quintus Horatius Flaccus (65 to 8 BCE) was one of the great lyric poets of the Roman era. Unlike the aristocratic Greek monodists, Horace did not grow up in affluent surroundings; instead, his father was an ex-slave, quite possibly an Italian enslaved during Rome's conflicts with other Italian city states during the early first century BCE. From what we can piece together of Horace's life (which is largely drawn from his own poetry – always a hazardous undertaking), his father was socially ambitious for his son, provided him with a good education in Rome and sent him to Athens to study philosophy. He thus received the sort of education that was not untypical for members of Rome's social élite. Unfortunately, Horace chose the losing side in the civil war, fighting with Brutus and Cassius at the Battle of Philippi (42 BCE) against Mark Antony and Octavius. His allegiance to the republicans meant the confiscation of his family property in Italy. Horace's poetry was therefore, as he portrays it, born out of his poverty and it provided the means of his social advancement and material prosperity. Through his poetry he came to the attention of Maecenas, an influential statesman and advisor of Augustus. Maecenas was one of the great literary patrons of the age and it was his financial support of Horace that allowed the poet to produce his verses in relative affluence. Maecenas provided Horace with a small estate in the Italian countryside to the north-east of Rome (the remains of which are currently being excavated).

Horace wrote a variety of poetic works including the *Epodes*, *Satires* and *Epistles*, but what might be considered his central work was his collection of lyric poetry: his *Odes* or *Carmina*. This major collection of three books with 88 poems in total was published in 23 BCE (he later added a fourth book). Horace presented himself as the first true Latin lyric poet. It was perhaps a tendentious claim; others, like Catullus (see Section 4.5 of this block and CD4, 'Poetic voices, political worlds', Tracks 1–25), had composed lyric Latin poems before him, but he was the first to produce a sustained collection consisting of only lyric pieces following the rhythms of the Greek masters. In the spirit of lyric poetry, Horace's *Odes* cover a vast variety of topics: celebration, love, friendship, politics, and what we might call a general philosophising on life and how to live it.

Ancient and modern lyric

Exercise

Think for just a moment about what the word 'poetry' means to you.

Discussion

If your thoughts are on the sort of poetry you have read so far on the course, then you will be thinking about epic, tragedy and comedy. However, think about what the term 'poetry' meant to you *before* your recent studies of ancient Greek poetry. The sort of poem that is most likely to come into the head of someone nowadays is what would be termed a 'lyric poem'. This usually means a fairly short poem that expresses the intense emotional mood of a single speaker. This type of lyric poetry is by far the largest category of verse in the modern world (narrative and dramatic verse being marginal in our society).

Although modern (lyric) poetry can incorporate almost any metrical form and virtually any subject, there is, nevertheless, an expectation that we will be reading the intense emotional meditations of an individual: an almost cathartic outpouring of feeling. It is published and in the public domain, but we still read as though we are peeking in at an essentially private train of thought. It is a process of overhearing rather than being directly addressed, and this is a big difference between *our* experience of lyric poetry and that of an *ancient* audience. Latin lyric poetry occupies a kind of middle position between the public performance of ancient Greek lyric and the private reflective experience of reading modern lyric.

Exercise

For an example of a modern lyric poem, look at Tony Harrison's 'Book End II' in Reading 3.24. You don't need to study this poem for the course but it gives you a good idea of the nature of modern lyric poetry; it articulates some powerful feelings of loss, loneliness and death; the 'I' of the poem sets out his thoughts and feelings without addressing them to anyone in particular.

RB

Then turn to Horace's 'Ode 3.6' in Reading 3.25 (a) (*Delicta maiorum* in English). Read through the translation of the poem fairly quickly while thinking about the following questions:

- Who is the poem addressed to?

- Is this an outpouring of personal feeling that the reader is overhearing, or is it a publicly directed address?

- What do you think the poem supposes is the role of the poet in society?

Discussion

Horace's lyric poetry is still very much a form of verse that presupposes, or actually includes, a named addressee. So in 'Ode 3.6' the poet speaks directly to a 'Roman' (i.e. an individual Roman who stands in the poem as the representative of the general Roman community). This creates an impression of dynamic interchange which gives this form of poetry a feeling of dialogue; or perhaps more precisely, it evokes the mood of a public forum rather than one of intimate subjective revelation. Thus for Horace, poetry could still be viewed as a matter of public instruction and edification. According to this model, the poet ought to be a sort of instructive mouthpiece for his community. The word that Horace uses to describe himself in his lyric poetry is *vates* – not a simple word to translate as it has a wide range of meanings: 'bard', 'priest' or 'prophet'. It does give us a good sense, however, of how Horace viewed his poetry as providing an edifying public voice for his community.

Case study: Horace, 'Ode 3.6'

The sequence of poems at the beginning of Horace's third book of *Odes* is often known as the 'Roman Odes'; we will turn again now to the last poem in this sequence as a case study of Horace's lyric poetry.

Formal properties of the poem

Exercise

Look again at 'Ode 3.6' in Reading 3.25 (a) and (b) and consider how the Latin poem and the English translation are set out on the page.

Discussion

You will have noticed that the poem is set out in a series of four-line units. This particular verse structure is known as 'Alcaic' after the Greek lyric poet, Alcaeus, the supposed inventor of this particular form of poetry. It is the most common metre in Horace's *Odes*: 33 out of the 88 poems in his first three books of the *Odes* – including all the 'Roman Odes' – are in this metre. Horace tends to use this metrical scheme when he wishes to impart a dignified air to his verse. You will also have noticed (in the original Latin) that when this metre is set out in a stanza, it looks like two longer lines followed by two shorter lines; in Alcaic verse the first two lines each have eleven syllables, the third line nine syllables and the fourth line ten syllables. In this manner each line is made up of a set pattern (with small variations allowed) of long and short syllables; these lines then combine to form a four-line stanza and then the pattern is repeated. This produces a distinctive look and sound. It is not so easy to capture all this when the Latin is translated into English, and so it is always as well to bear in mind when reading Horace's poetry in translation that what he writes is fitted to a precise rhythmical scheme, and that this in itself is an impressive achievement.

The stanza units of four lines can serve as self-contained sense units, but Horace quite typically allows his thought to run across stanzas rather than being contained within each one. Although each stanza can serve as a natural division in the sense of a poem, larger-scale patterns are also possible; for instance, I think that 'Ode 3.6' divides more naturally, in terms of the sense of the whole poem, into three divisions of four stanzas rather than into twelve individual stanzas.

This is the sort of technical information that you will not be able to bring to an initial reading of a Latin poet in translation. However, this additional knowledge can help us appreciate the artistry that goes into the composition of a poem and can provide clues as to the sort of effects that the poet is striving to put across to his reader.

Exercise

So that you can hear what 'Ode 3.6' sounds like in the original Latin and in the Alcaic metre, we have recorded a reading of the first part of the poem followed by its translation on CD4, Tracks 34 and 36. Take a moment now to listen to the recording.

Then read through Alfred Tennyson's tribute to Milton, 'In Quantity – Milton', which was also composed in Alcaic verse (Reading 3.26). This poem gives you a good idea of the grandiose effects that the Alcaic stanza can produce when incorporated into the English language. (There is no need to study the content of Tennyson's poem for the course: it is provided solely give you a sense of the sound and effect of the Alcaic metre before proceeding to the analysis of Horace's poem below.)

Content of the poem

Let us turn now from the form of the poem to its contents.

Exercise

Read through the whole of 'Ode 3.6' in Reading 3.25 (a) again. Then read through the first four stanzas more slowly. As you read, make notes on what you think the poet is saying here. Take note too of any references that you do not understand.

Discussion

Stanzas 1–4

The theme of the poem is set out clearly in the first stanza: the present generation of Romans must atone for the sins of their ancestors. The opening phrase might also suggest a theme of unwarranted suffering:

why, after all, should you be held responsible for the sins of your ancestors? We are then introduced to the specific nature of the sins the poet has in mind, and also to what he sees as the solution. The continuing problem is the neglect of Rome's temples and cult statues; the solution is to repair them. I'd say therefore that the opening of the poem suggests that the poet is expressing a need for pious behaviour. The present generation of Romans may not have caused this desecration, but unless they put it right they will be implicated in its consequences.

The poet then sets about expanding on his initial theme and drawing out a coherent framework of cause and effect. You will probably have noticed how the poet draws a direct link between Roman success and Roman piety, and again between neglect of the gods and loss, failure and suffering. The Romans may have felt a need at this time for an explanation or a way of coming to terms with the awful chaos and bloodshed of the civil wars. Why did the wars happen? What could be done to stop them happening again? One way to make sense of it all is to see everything in terms of the consequences of pious and impious behaviour. This might seem a reductive way of looking at the inevitably complicated events of history, but sometimes we all need the comfort of easy answers (and solutions).

As you read through the first stanzas of the poem you will probably have come across names and events which will be unfamiliar. In the second stanza, for instance, what the poet means by 'Hesperia' might not be immediately clear. It translates as 'land of the West' and it is used poetically to mean 'Italy'. This erudite and allusive trait of ancient poetry flourished in the Hellenistic period (336–331 BCE) and Horace was very much indebted to it. He didn't carry this to the excess that some Roman followers of these poetics did, but nevertheless his poetry can at times seem a little inaccessible to the modern reader.

You may also have noticed that there is a good deal of historical referencing going on that may not be familiar. The third stanza is full of historical detail. The reference to the bands of Monaeses and Pacorus and their defeat of ill-omened Roman offensives probably refer to the defeat of Crassus by the Parthians at Carrhae in 53 BCE, and the rout of one of Mark Antony's lieutenants in Parthia in 40 BCE. Equally plausibly, it could mean the rout of 40 BCE and the further loss of two more legions under another of Antony's generals in Parthia in 36 BCE. The references are not entirely clear even to a trained ancient historian; all we really know is that there is a reference here to

Roman defeats in Parthia. One imagines the historical details were more readily apparent to a Roman audience, though it is also likely that the theme of defeat in the east was more important than any historical precision.

In the fourth stanza Horace presents the vivid image of Rome besieged by insurrection and how this almost led to the destruction of the city by foreign forces. Here he undoubtedly refers to the last phase of the civil wars and the showdown between Octavius and Mark Antony (allied with Cleopatra) at the Battle of Actium in 31 BCE. The reference to Egypt must be to Cleopatra: in the Latin, the reference is actually to Ethiopia where many Egyptian slaves came from, many of whom doubtless manned the Egyptian fleet at Actium. Dacia was the name at the time for an area of the lower Danube; bowmen from Dacia served with Antony at Actium. This type of erudite detail reveals the debt Horace owes to Alexandrian poetics while placing it in a more immediate political and historical context.

In this way, Horace has shifted somewhat from the theme of impiety to that of civil strife, but he has already laid the foundation for the connection of one to the other. Civil strife has been the cause of religious neglect, but civil suffering has also been the result of such neglect. It is a vicious circle from which Rome must emerge and failure to do so could lead to ruin. A Rome that could dominate the world with the goodwill of the gods could similarly be destroyed by foreign powers if it alienated divine favour. You probably noticed that the language and allusion is highly compressed here: remember that poetry can (and often has to) pack a lot of meaning into a few words.

Exercise

Now carefully read stanzas 5–8 of 'Ode 3.6' (Reading 3.25). Again, note down the theme of these lines. How does this section relate to what has gone before? Are there any references that you don't understand?

RB

Discussion

Stanzas 5–8
These lines, you will have noticed, explore a different but related issue. So far, Horace has set out the theme of the need for the present generation of Romans to pay for the crimes of the past. These crimes have consisted of religious neglect, and the poet has then elaborated on the consequences of such neglect: the visitation of ruin on Rome in the form of failed military enterprises and potential destruction.

Having finished his opening train of thought, the poet then moves on to address the direct culpability of the present age. You can see here how Horace has shifted from a position in the opening stanza of what seems to be indirect guilt – atoning for the sins of those who came before – into one that highlights direct responsibility. Now the poet speaks of an age 'teeming with sin' (line 17). He draws a very stark picture of the present: a situation where sin has polluted marriage, children and households and in consequence disaster has overwhelmed Rome and its people. When you think about the tone of this passage you could well summon up the image of a fiery preacher berating the community he is part of and condemning its values and behaviour.

In the next three stanzas he elaborates on this image of a decadent Rome by painting a picture of sexual impropriety. A young woman is presented who enjoys learning exotic dances and gestures, and who is presented as longing for sinful sexual activity even before she is married. (Dancing was not a respectable activity for Roman women but rather the domain of actresses whose social rank in Rome was very low; you will notice that such activity is described as 'non-Roman', a decadent, foreign art from Asia Minor.) In a mounting crescendo of indignation, the poet then details her life after marriage. She seeks out young adulterers at the banquets of her husband with his knowledge and consent, making him her consort in marital prostitution. This is quite a picture of sexual immorality and one that is notably placed within the context of marriage.

Exercise

Now read stanzas 9–12 of 'Ode 3.6' (Reading 3.25 (a)). Make notes on how these lines develop the themes and argument of the preceding stanzas.

Discussion

Stanzas 9–12

As we move into the final third of the poem, Horace turns away from a graphic image of contemporary depravity into a contrasting picture of past virtue. The military failures that we saw earlier in the poem and the consequences of immoral and impious behaviour are now set against the military success of previous generations.

Unless you have a good grasp of Roman history you might have been a little lost with the references in the ninth stanza. 'Dyed the Punic sea with blood' (lines 33–34) is a reference to the Punic Wars (which were discussed in Part 1 of this block). More specifically, given the sea image, the reference is likely to be to the First Punic War (264–241 BCE) where the major battles were fought on water. The next reference is to Pyrrhus, a Greek king who fought against the Romans in a series of battles in southern Italy. (Although Pyrrhus was victorious, his losses were heavy: hence the phrase 'Pyrrhic victory'.) Antiochus was a king of Syria defeated by the Romans in 190 BCE. The most famous name here is Hannibal who led a Carthaginian force (including elephants) over the Alps and defeated the Romans on Italian soil several times over a number of years. Eventually he was forced to withdraw back to Carthage where he was finally defeated at the battle of Zama in 202 BCE. You don't need to worry about remembering all these historical details but it does give you a good idea of the sort of information that a Roman poet took for granted his original audience would know.

The point of these historical details is to build up a vivid contrast in the poem between then and now. The Roman young men of this age were of a different type altogether from the decadent youth of Horace's day; they were upright men born of upright parents. I think Horace indulges here in a little vignette of past rustic virtue, a celebration of what he sees as Rome's true primordial character.

The virtuous soldiers of Rome's past were farmers by profession; they fought in Rome's armies as a form of mobilised citizen militia in the days when Rome had no professional standing army. This is the image Horace wants to project as truly Roman – a hardy, virtuous, rustic race, brought up strictly to work the land. These honest-living countrymen are identified as 'Sabines' in Horace's poem. The Sabines were one of the many ancient peoples of Italy, living to the north-east of Rome (the same area where Horace lived on his estate); in later Roman culture they become a symbol of old-fashioned Italian virtue and simplicity. The poet here draws a deliberate contrast between this past agricultural society, the rural society from which Rome sprung, and the decadent, contemporary urban society he has shown the reader in the preceding stanzas.

In the last stanza of the poem, Horace brings together the themes of the poem in a generalised conclusion on the declining condition of the human race. Each past generation is characterised as in decline from the standards of the one that went before it, and so even the excesses of the present are set to be surpassed by those to come. This pessimistic idea of human progress – what we might call the 'grumpy old man' viewpoint – is a common one across many cultures and is often set down in moralising texts as a kind of wake-up call to the present generation to mend its ways. The less-than-chirpy conclusion serves well to reinforce the poet's gloomy assessment of the present, and by placing his diatribe on contemporary society in the last stanza within the context of a generalised truth, he seeks to give greater validity to his message. We might also consider that this mixing up of the particular and the general is often what makes poetry successful and its messages so forceful. The specifics of a certain situation (here Rome in the present as opposed to Rome in the past) are set within the wider picture of how the world is in general (decline from one age to the next). Specific contemporary details are proved by an appeal to the universal, and particular individual emotions are rendered more accessible by placing them in a more generalised context.

Context of the poem

Finally, let us think about the poem in the context of Augustus and the sort of policies he was pursuing at Rome.

Exercise

Read quickly through the whole poem again (Reading 3.25 (a)) and think about the following questions:

- How does Horace's subject matter fit into the context of Augustan Rome and the policies of Augustus that we studied earlier?

- How does it affect our impression of Horace's sincerity to know that he was directly dependent on the Augustan regime?

Discussion

I would be surprised if reading Horace's poem didn't make you think back to our earlier work on Augustus. As you read through the first two stanzas of the poem, you will probably have recalled that the need for religious revival was one of the central themes of the Augustan principate. Remember how Augustus in the *Res Gestae* boasted of his restoration of Rome's temples and the revival of religious rites and offices that were falling into disuse. Augustus himself was the chief priest of the Roman state, the *pontifex maximus*, and a member of virtually every other religious body. As we saw earlier, he portrayed himself as the saviour of the Roman state and this image was partially realised through his restoration of Rome's religious infrastructure. Thus the initial theme of this Ode, suggesting as it does a direct link between religious revival and Roman success, appears to be very much in line with the thinking and actions of the princeps himself.

This initial theme is developed in the third and fourth stanzas in line with Augustus' own way of thinking. The argument of the poem thus far is that religious neglect has caused misery and suffering for Rome, and this has been expressed in part through the defeat of Roman forces and the near destruction of the city by eastern powers. The obvious implication of this argument is that Roman success will be based on religious revival and the defeat of such foreigners. Foreign powers who have threatened Rome with potential destruction are ones that are expressly associated with defeat by Augustus.

As we noted in our discussion of the first four stanzas, the reference to the bands of Monaeses and Pacorus in stanza 3 probably refers to the defeat of Crassus by the Parthians at Carrhae in 53 BCE, and the losses suffered under Mark Antony's command in campaigns in Parthia during the years 40–36 BCE. Augustus' 'defeat' of the Parthians was a prominent theme of the early part of the Augustan principate. You will have noticed that I have put defeat in inverted commas: this is because it was not a military triumph but rather a negotiated diplomatic agreement in 20 BCE that saw the Parthians return the legionary standards lost during the defeats of Crassus' and Antony's generals. The event is mentioned by Augustus in the *Res Gestae* (where he rather dishonestly asserts that he compelled the Parthians to return the standards and become suppliants of the Roman people). Although this poem was probably written and published before the actual return of the standards in 20 BCE, it is quite probable that there was a great deal of hype about the necessity to do so before then.

The return of the standards became a potent symbol of Augustan triumph in both the art and on the coinage of the day (see Figure 3.25 below and Plate 44 in the Illustrations Book). You can see a kneeling Parthian with a standard depicted on a coin and then a close-up of the cuirass from the famous statue of Augustus known as the *prima porta*; the central scene shows a Parthian handing back a standard to a Roman general, often thought to be Augustus' son-in-law and the next princeps, Tiberius.

As we have seen above, the foreign powers in the fourth stanza refer specifically to the forces of Mark Antony and Cleopatra that Octavius defeated at Actium. Hence, Augustus is once again implicitly associated with righting the wrongs of Rome's past and setting the state in the right direction. Horace's alignment of Rome's decline with

Figure 3.25   Coin (reverse) of 19 BCE showing a kneeling Parthian with a Roman standard. The British Museum (BMC 58). © The Trustees of The British Museum.

threatening eastern powers accords with the sort of political rhetoric associated with the early part of the Augustan principate. For in the lead-up to the Battle of Actium, Octavius strove to present the conflict with Antony not as a civil war – a battle between Romans – but rather as a fight between west and east, a conflict between Roman values and oriental despotism. (You have already met this kind of constructed clash of values and cultures between west and east in Block 2 when studying the Greeks and Persians.) Cleopatra, not Mark Antony, is the figure who symbolises this conflict in Augustan literature, because she is the more potent symbol for the sort of cultural conflict for which Augustus wished this phase of the civil wars to be remembered. You will notice how Horace mirrors this sort of political spin: in the fourth stanza there is no hint that the conflict in question involved Romans fighting Romans. All we are allowed to see behind the allusive references are the threatening forces of eastern despotism.

As the poem develops into a tirade against contemporary morals in stanzas 5–8, it is easy once more to draw parallels with another major tenet of Augustus' principate: social and moral reform. Horace's poem again seems very much in tune with the types of immoral behaviour that the Augustan legislative programme was purportedly aimed at countering. Adultery and marriage were central issues in this legislative programme, and the image of sexual immorality and venality that Horace paints in this poem suggests quite clearly the need for Augustus' measures if Rome was to escape a vicious cycle of divine disapproval and its consequences. Again, Horace's poem most likely predates the actual legislation on adultery and marriage of 18 BCE, as in the case of the return of the Parthian standards: this probably tells us that this legislation too, and the mood that provoked it, were in the air for a while before the laws were passed (we shall revisit this issue below with reference to Propertius 2.7). Once more, though, it is clear that Horace's poem is very much in tune with central aspects of Augustus' political thinking.

In the last four stanzas we saw the privileging of a primitive past and the promotion of rural over urban values. A sort of romantic idealisation of rustic sensibility is also a prevalent Augustan theme (it finds its way into Augustan art, for instance, in the form of little idyllic pastoral vignettes, as in Colour Plate 16 of your Illustrations Book). It is one branch of an Augustan climate that sought to promote an image of Rome as a virtuous peasant society rather than a cosmopolitan city, and you can see how Horace's poem fits into this pattern. Augustus, too, you will remember, used himself and his family as paradigms of simplicity and sufficiency – wearing clothes made by the female members of his household and living without luxury and ostentation.

We might well ask, then, whether in the case of Horace and Augustus there was a meeting of like minds. Appearances would suggest a remarkable coincidence between the themes of Horace's poem (religious neglect, moral decadence, decline from the values of the past) and the moral tone of Augustus' own initiatives. Given that Horace was supported financially by a gift of a country estate from one of Augustus' close advisers, does this mean that the poet's fervour is mercenary righteous indignation? Is Horace a genuine moralist or a poetic toady? The question of autonomy is always an important one to bear in mind when dealing with financially dependent artists, but one might also consider that most great works of art have been produced in such circumstances. Certainly Horace had incentives to be favourable to the aims of Augustus, but at the same time we should not underestimate that Augustus' initiatives may well have tapped into some deep-seated contemporary feelings. The prolonged destruction of the civil wars required explanation; sense had to be made out of the chaos of the world. A belief that over-indulgence and decadence had precipitated – and could continue to precipitate – disaster was a potential answer and one in line with the moralistic tendencies of ancient historical thinking, as you have seen earlier in the block in the writings of Sallust and Livy. Augustus may have exploited the situation to indulge his own penchant for conservatism; Horace may have taken his money and said what he thought he should; but they may also have both sincerely believed in the need for such change.

Summary

Looking back at Horace's poem, there is a lot to talk about. We can, when approaching this type of poem, concentrate on various aspects. At one level the poem can be appreciated for its formal properties: for instance, the way in which the poet has fitted his Latin words to the rhythm of the Greek metre (difficult though this is to grasp in translation). We could also admire the way he has arranged his poem; we have remarked, for instance, on how the poem is divided into units of four lines that match the original metrical units and we have also analysed the poem in three units of four stanzas which correspond to three major sense units in the poem. The first four stanzas introduce the themes of atonement, religious neglect and its consequences; the next four paint a portrait of contemporary sexual decadence; and the last four show a contrasting image of past rural simplicity that runs into a moralising conclusion about declining standards. Horace's poems are put together metrically with almost mathematical precision and his content is tightly structured.

Apart from this formal appreciation of Horace's poetic craft, we can also read Horace's poem on a more historical level, as a poetic document of a particular moment in Roman culture. When we read the poem in this manner we move beyond a formal appreciation of the beauty of the poem and the artistry that went into its creation and focus on the content of the poem; we then move from the content to the wider cultural and historical backdrop that frames its composition. When we read in this way we can start to see how a poem is implicated in, and contributes to, the debates of its day. What had caused the ruinous civil strife that had afflicted Rome? What was the way forward from here? What can we do to make sure we don't go through this again? Here the voice of the poet expresses the concerns of his community; it berates and shames his community, inciting repentance and change in a fiery prophetic tone.

Poetry and history can make fascinating bedfellows and the power of poetry often lies in its attempt to entwine individual experience of the world into wider patterns of general and universal principles. Poetry, we might say, incorporates historical detail, and tries to make its significance more than simply tied to a single passing moment. This can be, and often is, a political act to some degree. Horace's poem demonstrates well how poetry can participate in the political climate of a culture.

5.4   Roman elegiac poetry

For our second section on Augustan poetry we turn now from Horatian lyric to a different type of poetry: elegy. If you have the time, you might like to do the following optional reading here.

- *OCCC* entry on 'elegiac poetry, Greek'
- *OCCC* entry on 'elegiac poetry, Latin'

Greek elegiac poetry

Elegiac poetry is another ancient verse form dating back to at least the seventh century BCE. It is a form of lyric poetry made up of elegiac couplets. Each of these couplets consists of a **hexameter** (a line of verse with six metrical units made up of long and short syllables) and a **pentameter** (a line of verse with five similar but not identical metrical units). (See 'The form of epic in Section 5.5 of this block.) When a hexameter and pentameter are combined in this manner they give an effect like the following:

> Down in a deep dark dell sat an old sow munchin' a beanstalk.
>   Out of her mouth came forth grunts of a greedy delight

(Anon.)

This is more elegantly expressed in Coleridge's imitation of Ovid's elegiac verse:

> In the Hexameter rises the fountain's silvery column,
>   In the pentameter aye falling in melody back.

(Coleridge, *Ovidian Elegiac Metre*)

Exercise

A little later in this part of the block, you will be looking at a case study of an example of Roman elegy: a poem by Propertius. We have recorded a reading of the beginning of 'Propertius 2.7' and its translation on CD4, Tracks 43 and 45. Listen to this recording now to get a sense of the sound and rhythm of elegiac poetry.

The origins of this type of verse are disputed. The name 'elegy' most likely has its origins in the ancient Greek word for a lament, but Greek elegiac poetry itself, though it includes laments, was used for a wide variety of purposes. In a shortened form, usually called 'epigram' and often distinguished as a separate poetic form, elegiac verse was originally used for dedications and funeral inscriptions but it later developed into a more free-ranging genre.

In Archaic Greece, elegy, like lyric, was composed for performance in a social setting and was probably also accompanied by a musical instrument, the *aulos* (a type of oboe mentioned in Block 2). The themes of elegy from Archaic Greece vary considerably: they can be exhortations to military valour, diatribes on the political situation, poems on wine, women (and boys) and song, or more personal reflections and philosophising on life in general. Therefore elegy was, in its ancient Greek form, a social form of poetry that admitted a wide variety of use. The categorisation of such poetry as elegy appears to have been more due to its choice of metre than its content per se. This variety of use continued through the Greek Hellenistic period but the original social setting of this poetry (as with lyric) was lost. Hellenistic elegiac poems tend to have longer erudite mythological narratives.

Elegy from ancient to modern

Our notion of elegy is somewhat different from the models from ancient Greece. When we think of elegy we tend to think in terms of laments: poems that express a melancholic reflection on life and death in general.

If you have the time, you might like to do some optional reading here. There are two famous examples of elegy reprinted in reader 2, and the full texts of these poems are included on the course website. The poems are:

- Shelley's 'Adonais' (1821) in Reading 3.27
- Thomas Gray's 'Elegy Written in a Country Churchyard' (1751) in Reading 3.28

Shelley's poem is a lament in memory of the English poet, John Keats; Gray's poem is more of a general meditation on life and death. Though both these poems would be classed as elegies, neither of them is written in elegiac couplets; rather both are written in iambic pentameters, the most common form of metre in English verse. Gray's poem consists of four-line stanzas of iambic pentameters with a rhyming scheme of *abab* (i.e. the first and third lines and the second and fourth lines rhyme with each other). Shelley's poem consists of a variant known as Spenserian metre (after the poet Edmund Spenser, author of *The Faerie Queene*); this is a more elaborate scheme of nine-line stanzas, eight lines of iambic pentameters and a final line of hexameter, in a rhyming scheme of *ababbcbcc*. You don't need to remember these specific points or study the details of the poems; they are simply provided for reference and enjoyment and to allow you to compare modern poetic examples to the ancient ones we are studying.

The nature of Roman elegy

Let us now turn to our main focus for this section: Roman elegy. Elegiac poetry (in the form of epigram) first appeared at Rome in the second century BCE, mostly in the form of short erotic pieces composed by Roman aristocrats for amusement in their leisure hours. It is, however, in the late republic and early principate that elegy really flourished at Rome. You have already encountered the poetry of Catullus in your work in Section 4.5 of this block (and on CD4, Tracks 1–25). Catullus wrote in a great variety of lyric metres, including elegiac couplets. Some of his poems in elegiac couplets are very short and more in the tradition of epigram than elegy, but a few are lengthier and more in keeping with the later Roman elegiac tradition.

The poet who probably established the genre of Roman elegy in Rome was Cornelius Gallus, a prominent statesman during the early years of the Augustan principate. Gallus was the first Roman governor of Egypt but his ambition and celebration of his achievements led to his recall and the suspicion of Augustus, and he committed suicide (*c.*26 BCE). Gallus wrote four books of elegiac poetry, probably titled *Amores* ('Loves') but virtually none of his work survives. In fact until 1978 we only knew of one pentameter of his verse, but in that year a further nine lines came to light on a bit of preserved papyrus recovered from a rubbish dump at a Roman fort by the River Nile in Egypt.

The poets whose works have become most synonymous with Roman elegy were those writing in the Augustan period: Propertius, Tibullus and Ovid. The work of these poets, published probably over a span of twenty years or so, represents the zenith of this poetic form in Latin literature. (Ovid's poetic output was prolific but here we will only be dealing with his *Amores*, the three-book collection that he wrote in the mainstream tradition of Roman elegy.)

If you have the time, you might like to do some optional reading here, and look at the following entries in OCCC.

- *OCCC* entry on 'Propertius'
- *OCCC* entry on 'Tibullus'
- *OCCC* entry on 'Ovid'

Themes in Roman elegy

Now let us consider some short excerpts from a number of elegiac poems by Propertius, Tibullus and Ovid.

Exercise

Read through the excerpts below and make notes on what you see as some common themes.

You will notice that the excerpts are set out with the second line indented from the first. This reflects in translation the form of the Latin verse with the longer hexameter line followed by a shorter pentameter line. (You can find the full Latin text of a Roman elegy,

'Propertius 2.7', in Reading 3.29 which we will use for our case study in this section.) All translations are my own.

Propertius

I am not concerned with reputation, nor was born suited for military service,
    rather fate wants me to undergo my own type of martial service.

      (Propertius 1.6.29–30)

Love is a god of peace, we lovers worship peace,
    Let my hard battles be with my mistress.

      (Propertius 3.5.1–2)

In love I either want to be in pain or to hear one in pain,
    either to see my tears or yours ...

      (Propertius 3.8.23–24)

Medicine cures all human pains:
    Love alone cares not for a doctor of its disease.

      (Propertius 2.1.57–58)

For me it is not right to love another, nor to break off from this woman;
    Cynthia was the first, Cynthia will be the last.

      (Propertius 1.12.19–20)

He is mistaken, who seeks to impose a limit on mad passion:
    true love doesn't know how to have any boundary.

      (Propertius 2.15.29–30)

Tibullus

And so I see slavery and a mistress ready for me,
    now it's farewell for me to my ancestral freedom.
Grim slavery is for me and I am held by chains
and Love that never slackens the bonds of a wretched man.

      (Tibullus 2.4.1–4)

Let us, Delia, be a paradigm of love when our hair is both white.

      (Tibullus 1.6.85–86)

Ovid

Every lover is a soldier ...

> (Ovid 1.9.1)

Why biting envy do you cast in my face the charge of idle years,
    and call my poetry the work of a slothful intellect;
complaining that I don't in the traditional manner,
    while the vigorous years of life allow,
pursue the dusty rewards of military service, nor learn the wordy laws,
    nor prostitute my voice in the thankless forum.

> (Ovid 1.15.1–6)

Review your notes before reading the following discussion.

Discussion

You will probably have noticed in the excerpts above a number of recurring themes:

- a rejection of war and military service but an embrace of love as an alternate form of military venture;

- love as an almost masochistic experience and one akin to slavery;

- love as an incurable, irresistible and enduring force;

- a rejection of conventionally valued activity.

Although Roman elegy is far from uniform in its content, it does display a unity of sorts in its general subject matter – love – and you will often see the poetry of the Augustan elegists referred to as 'Latin love elegy'. Its engagement with the theme of love was, however, rather idiosyncratic. Certain norms and conventions for this type of poetry were probably already in place by the time Tibullus, Propertius and Ovid were writing. We are a little restricted in our knowledge of the expectations a Roman reader might have brought to the experience of reading this type of poetry by the loss of so much of Gallus' poetry in particular. However, although the debt that the Augustan elegists owed to their predecessors is hard to determine, we can certainly define certain broad characteristics of this sort of poetry from the work of Ovid, Propertius and Tibullus. Roman love elegy embraces a form of love that is expressed as an unfulfilling, masochistic subjugation to an imperious female figure. In Latin, this figure is called *domina* (mistress); the word appears in the odd lines of Gallus that we do possess. This form of poetry is also typically characterised by complaint (one might almost say of constant whinging) and at this level it does indeed link to the origin of the Greek genre in lament.

The theme of subjugation is explored in one of the major metaphors of Roman elegy: *servitium amoris* (the slavery of love). *Domina* in Latin can have a technical meaning of female slave-owner. It should be borne in mind that this metaphor was quite bold in a society whose economy was based on slave labour and where there were a high proportion of slaves in the population. This gives an added dimension to what otherwise may be thought of as a hackneyed analogy for the experience of being in love.

Another major metaphor in this type of poetry is *militia amoris* (the 'military service of love'). Again, this is perhaps a bit more than a purely conventional metaphor in a society where warfare was traditionally carried out by a citizen militia. We can say that these two metaphors attempt to translate the sphere of love into the terms of central aspects of ancient Roman experience. This equation of one type of experience with another is, of course, a prime characteristic of analogy and metaphor; it is an attempt to make sense of one thing by comparing it to another. The extent, though, to which this may be considered challenging – or indeed shocking – depends on just how different from each other the things being compared are. Roman love elegy, for example, seems to engage in a deliberate strategy of shock and provocation. It does this by taking an area of activity that, to a conventional Roman way of thinking, was frivolous and marginal – love – and elevating it to a central importance that would be quite unacceptable to the 'moral majority' of Roman society. By taking this stance, the central male figure in this type of poetry demonstrates an aversion to public life and his civic duties and instead immerses himself in an egocentric pursuit of a woman who appears constantly to reject him and make his life miserable. From the conventional ethical standpoint of Roman aristocratic society (the Roman elegists, unlike Horace, almost certainly all belonged to the higher social ranks of Roman society from birth), this behaviour is shameless and unacceptable. Roman male aristocrats were expected to be born leaders who embraced their civic duty and strove to excel in state-related activity.

Roman love elegy thus appears to profess a lifestyle, and points of view, that seem directly contrary to conventional Roman morality. The narrators of this type of poetry all present themselves as young men, and it is tempting therefore to see in Roman love elegy a sort of youthful rebellion and a counter-cultural movement that defines itself in terms that are deliberately provocative and designed to offend conventional sensibilities.

Case study: 'Propertius 2.7'

So far we have looked at the background to Roman elegy and at some of its characteristics by considering some excerpts from different poems. Let's now turn to a reading of a whole elegy in more detail.

Exercise

Read through the translation of 'Propertius 2.7' in Reading 3.29. As you read, jot down some notes for yourself on the following questions:

- What do you think this poem is about?

- How would you describe the attitudes of the narrator?

- Is the image that the narrator projects for himself in keeping with the sorts of policies that Augustus was trying to promote?

Discussion

What this poem is about precisely may seem a little difficult to pin down. Don't worry: you are not alone here. It is clear that some law has been removed and that this is a cause of celebration for the narrator and his *domina*, Cynthia. Given that the poem goes on to talk about their potential separation in terms of brides and husbands, we must surely be right in thinking that this poem is connected somehow to the Augustan legislation on marriage. Yet this idea has caused confusion in that this poem should be dated to the 20s BCE (the last datable reference in Propertius' Book 2 is to 26 BCE) but the legislation on marriage did not appear until 18 BCE. Again, as in the case with Horace's lyric poem we looked at earlier, this may tell us that the legislation was being enforced in some way earlier than its passage into law. Another possibility is that the poem refers to a quite different but related piece of legislation. Some have argued that this poem alludes not to the measures that would eventually be codified in the 18 BCE law, but rather to measures Octavius introduced before the Battle of Actium in order to raise money for his military campaign (the measure in question here was a tax on bachelors that was repealed later in 28 BCE). So you can see that the precise details of ancient history are often impossible to recover; trying to unravel the historical references of poems can be equally problematic. All that we can be sure of here is that this poem presents the removal of some legislation that the narrator saw as getting in the way of his lifestyle.

Exercise

Having considered the general context, let's move on to the content of the poem and analyse it more closely. I have divided my own thoughts into three sections:

1   Lines 1–6

2   Lines 7–14

3   Lines 15–20

Reread each of these sections again before looking at the discussion below.

Discussion

1   *Lines 1–6*

The poem opens with Cynthia celebrating at the repeal of a law, the terms of which she and the narrator had both spent some time weeping over in case it should separate them. As discussed above, the exact nature and terms of this law are unclear. The lack of precise detail does not, however, detract from interpreting the mood and sense of the poem. Whether or not this refers to an early version of the Augustan laws on marriage or something else, it evokes a context of state intervention in lifestyle choices. The reaction of the narrator and his *domina* at the time was of despair, which was replaced with joy at the removal of the threat. However, the recollection of the couple's feelings quickly gives way in the poem to a more belligerent and confrontational stance. The narrator is not going to take this lying down: the power of love cannot be easily thwarted. Jupiter (the supreme Roman god) himself could not divide lovers who don't wish it. This defiant stance in the area of love is typical of elegy. Love is the force that controls everything and which can't be resisted; love in elegy, unlike in the world outside it, must be given primacy over all else.

Mention of Jupiter and his inability to part lovers moves straight into a parallel reference to 'Caesar'. Caesar here is Octavius; as we saw earlier, Octavius gained the use of this name after his posthumous adoption by Julius Caesar; it later became part of the official name that every princeps adopted. The poem moves forward from Jupiter to Octavius in a logically parallel fashion;

Jupiter is the most powerful of the gods, Caesar the most powerful man. However, the parallel is not entirely flattering, for it already presupposes defeat for Octavius. If the greatest god cannot part unwilling lovers, how can a man? Although Caesar is introduced in suitably honorific terms (he is 'great'), his greatness is soon qualified; his power lies in his military might, but military power, the narrator asserts, is of no use in the province of love. Here we can see elegy's typical demarcation of the areas of love and war and of public and private life. The narrator in effect denies Octavius the legitimacy to intervene in his life.

2   *Lines 7–14*

In these lines the narrator continues his defiant stance and further outlines his personal opposition to marriage and war. He says he would sooner die (strong language, but remember elegy is typically full of histrionics) than abandon Cynthia for marriage. In a bold inversion the narrator imagines his marriage as a type of funeral, an event to be dreaded rather than celebrated; the roles of husband and wife are presented as the very antithesis of what he and his *domina* desire. In the context of a climate of moral and social conservatism that Octavius/Augustus represented, these are pretty powerful statements. The Augustan laws were expressly designed to promote marriage among Rome's élite as a moral and civic necessity; the narrator's rejection of this call appears uncompromising. The refusal of marriage turns again here, as at the end of the first section of the poem, into a rejection of war. This is also expressed in very strong terms; the poet denies that it is his function to provide sons for war; the elegist's role is to be a lover rather than a warrior. But at the same time as such sentiments may seem conventional, they are also expressed with tremendous force and in such a manner that it is difficult not to see this as political invective.

3   *Lines 15–20*

In the last section of this poem, the narrator expands on the theme of his own form of military campaigning: his erotic life with Cynthia. Here we see a treatment of the theme of *militia amoris* that we discussed above. This theme grows naturally out of the thought and progression of the poem and its embrace of love and rejection of war. The elegist sets up his own erotic sphere as the privileged one; amorous rather than military warfare is the true measure; the glory of the elegist isn't derived from conventional military exploits but through his own elegiac brand of fighting; elegy sets its own standards for distinction that are defined precisely by their contrast to societal norms.

The manner in which the poem ends reinforces this idiosyncratic and egocentric perspective. Cynthia, the *domina*, is all that matters to the elegist; his world is contained and fulfilled within this horizon; love of her is more important, he says, than being a father. You will notice here how this final couplet also picks up another theme of the Augustan legislative programme: procreation. The necessity of producing heirs is also anathema to the elegiac perspective; it only has eyes for its own erotically compulsive behaviour.

In these last few lines there are also a couple of mythical and erudite references. Castor (line 16) was the legendary son of the Spartan king Tyndareus and Leda, and along with his twin brother, Pollux, he forms the unit known as the *Gemini* (twins) or *Dioscuri* (Helen of Troy was their sister). The Borysthenes in line 18 were those who lived by the River Borysthenes, a river in Scythia flowing to the Black Sea. This sort of detail points to the conscious artistry of elegy: it would be a mistake to read this poetry as spontaneous expression. Chances are that Propertius did not come up with the Latin word Borysthenidas at the end of a pentameter on the spur of the moment.

Summary

We see then in 'Propertius 2.7' many of the salient themes of Roman love elegy that we considered earlier: the primacy of love; love as an end in itself; a love of peace and an opposition to war; a controversial and confrontational dialogue with moral and social convention. The narrator in this poem seems to project an image of himself as a young radical whose protestations point to an impassioned rejection of the authoritarian politics of the Augustan principate. Certainly the poem appears to strike a pose of defiant opposition to the idea of legislation on marriage and procreation, the cornerstones of the Augustan programme.

Roman elegy: some further considerations

Counter-cultural or conformist?

We have just seen the narrator present himself in fairly radical terms in 'Propertius 2.7'. However, before we start to think of the elegiac narrator as some sort of angry young rebel, let's take a look at some more passages from elegy and see how the narrator presents himself in these extracts.

Read the following extracts and think about how the narrator appears to view his own behaviour. (Again, these extracts are my own translations.)

Propertius

Cynthia first captured wretched me with her eyes,
  I whom no desire had yet contaminated.
Then Love cast down my look of stubborn pride and
  pressed my head under his feet, until the scoundrel taught me
to hate decent girls and to live my life with no reason.
  Ah me, for a whole year now this madness has not let up.

  (Propertius 1.1.1–7)

Nature has given a vice to everyone at birth: fortune allotted
  to me the fault of always being in love.

  (Propertius 2.22A.17–18)

But if now Cynthia were to look upon me kindly,
  I would not be called the fount of worthlessness,
nor in this manner would my bad reputation be paraded through
    Rome.

  (Propertius 2.24.5–7)

Venus had taken hold of me and was roasting me in a savage
    cauldron;
  I was bound with my hands tied behind my back. But look! My
garlanded ship
has reached the harbour, the Syrtes [treacherous sandbanks] are past
    and
 my anchor has been cast. Now, finally, weary from the vast tide, I have
regained my senses, and my wounds have healed into sanity. Good
    Sense,
if you are a goddess, I dedicate myself in your sanctuary.

  (Propertius 3.24.14–20)

I was a laughing stock among the banquets when the tables were set in
  place, and anyone was free to gossip about me.

  (Propertius 3.25.1–2)

Ovid

I am that Naso[1] the poet of my own depravity.

(Ovid 2.1.2)

I would not dare to defend my own faulty way of life, nor
   to set in motion fraudulent arms against my faults. I confess
(if there is any good in confessing one's faults); and having
   confessed them like a mad man I attack them. I hate the way
that I am but though I want not to be that way I'm powerless not to be;
   Alas, how hard it is to carry the weight you are eager to set aside.

(Ovid 2.4.1–6)

If there is anyone who thinks it is shameful to be a slave to a girl
   I shall be convicted as shameful in that man's judgement!
Yet let me be considered disreputable provided that Venus may
   burn me with a more gentle flame.

(Ovid 2.17.1–3)

Discussion

In these extracts the narrators seem to display an acknowledgment of their deviant and shameful lifestyle and behaviour. How then do we respond to these open acknowledgements of misconduct? Is this a case of pursuing a lifestyle and not caring about how one will be judged by the rest of society, or is it a realisation by the narrator of aberrant behaviour that he feels unable to stop? In other words, does the narrator embrace his shame willingly or under coercion; is his profession of shame ironic or sincere? The last two Propertian extracts above from poems 3.24 and 3.25 perhaps give us some insight into these questions. These poems come right at the end of Book 3 and were probably the last poems in Propertius' original collection (this is by no means certain, but there are echoes in poem 3.24 of poem 1.1, which suggest they serve as bookends to the collection).

---

[1] Ovid's full Latin name is Publius Ovidius Naso.

Exercise

Quickly reread the extracts above from Propertius 3.24 and 3.25 and then proceed to the discussion below.

Discussion

As you read these extracts you probably felt that the narrator was happy to see the back of his past elegiac existence. He says that he is emerging from madness into sanity and that his days of being an object of ridicule are behind him. In this manner the Propertian narrative seems to come full circle from the narrator's erotic capture and lapse into erotic madness in poem 1.1 (and also in the extracts above) to his emergence from erotic folly in 3.24–25. Ultimately, you may feel that this actually gives this type of poetry a conservative, rather than radical, feel. The elegiac viewpoint on such a reading could be seen as one that is ultimately presented as flawed; it is a narrative of youthful foolishness that the narrator finally puts behind him. In this sense, the world of Roman elegy is like a period of youthful experimentation and excess, which most cultures accept as a normal transitional phase; a sort of societal safety valve, a carnival for the young designed to blow off steam before the acceptance of one's adult responsibilities.

This might give us a rather different perspective on poems such as 'Propertius 2.7'. Perhaps in this poem the reader is being invited not to admire the feistiness of a young rebel but mock the ludicrous and shameful posturing of an obviously misguided adolescent. In this case, the depiction of the elegiac narrator could, in fact, be seen as providing support for the Augustan legislation; obviously, such laws were needed to put young men like the Propertian narrator back on the tracks. After all, the elegiac narrator in poems 3.24 and 3.25 himself seems to confess that he has been acting like an idiot.

We must remember, however, that readers can be difficult to control and even if the intentions of the elegiac author were to portray the antics of his narrator as delinquent youthful behaviour, there is still no guarantee that a reader would necessarily read the poems that way. A Roman reader might have chosen to identify with the viewpoints and values of the elegiac narrator rather than reject them, and a last-minute disclaimer in the final poems of the collection might not have dissuaded him or her.

Sincerity and subjectivity in Roman elegy

At this point, let us think a little bit more about the notions of sincerity and subjectivity in poetry. It is probably fair to say that most of us, when we read modern poetry, tend to assume that the 'I' speaking in the poem is the author, and that what is being said represents the author's own feelings and beliefs at some level or another (unless there is something that specifically tells us otherwise). In other words, we presuppose some degree of sincere expression; we don't perhaps expect that an author's poems are a straightforward window into their life – poetry is not autobiography – but neither do we generally expect that the 'I' of a poem has nothing at all to do with its author.

Ancient poetry tends not to be subjective in this same manner; nor does it generally value poetry as the outpouring of intensely sincere feeling in the same way. Modern poetry, we might say, places the emphasis on the link between a poet's actual experience and his or her heartfelt expression of it. Ancient poetry, on the other hand, is more concerned with the ties that bind an author and a reader together; one could say that it is a poetics of plausible expectation and that sincerity here is more of a contrived artistic effect than a benchmark of how well a poet has transposed personal experience into art.

Different genres of ancient poetry (satire, lyric, elegy) tend to follow certain conventions. This applies not only to situations and settings but also to the characterisation of the narrator. In other words, a reader may well have come to a piece of ancient poetry with certain expectations based solely on what genre the poem belonged to, and he or she would also have had a sense of what sort of character the narrator was likely to be. This idea of writing in character is often referred to as the author assuming a *persona*, a mask; the word derives from the masks used by different characters in the ancient Greek theatre. (You have already encountered this notion of *personae* with regard to the poetry of Homer, Hesiod and Sappho in Essay Three, 'Sing Muse: authorial voices in early Greek poetry', which you read in conjunction with Block 1).

Different ancient genres presuppose different *personae* for their narrators. If we applied this concept to Roman elegy we would then consider that the narrator of the elegies, the elegiac *persona* as distinct from the actual author, could be characterised as a young, love-besotted dilettante, but that we should in no way confuse the characterisation of this *persona* with the actual Roman author. In other words, Ovid may in reality have been an extremely dull family man, but his elegiac *persona* in contrast is a sharp, witty, morally dubious young man-about-town.

An approach to literature based on *personae* can serve as a necessary corrective to a tendency to assume that the words of a poet are a direct reflection of an author's opinions, feelings or life in general. Roman elegy, for instance, like Horatian lyric, is very sophisticated. It can contain erudite mythological references, and the difficult process of fitting the content to the metre in itself tends to work against a direct spontaneous outpouring of emotion, which in any case is a Romantic ideal (i.e. one belonging to the late eighteenth/early nineteenth centuries) rather than a Classical one. A Roman reader, it could be argued, would have enjoyed the antics of this elegiac *persona* without giving any thought to any possible connection between this character and its author.

There is a danger, though, in making this kind of neat division, and perhaps particularly so in the case of elegy. In this specific genre the name of the narrator in the text and the actual author outside it are the same: the author uses his own name in his poetry. This could, of course, serve merely to provide a bit more of a tease to a sophisticated audience, an added level of piquancy in the *persona*/author division. However, it is also possible that elegy deliberately tried to elide the division between *persona* and author and so suggested a connection between the Roman in the text and the one outside it; after all, they both went by the same name. This sort of confusion of art and life is precisely what the Ovidian narrator complains about in *Amores* 3.12.

Exercise

Read the excerpts from *Amores* 3.12 below (my own translations). As you read, consider what the narrator is saying about the relationship between a poet and his audience.

She who just now was called mine, whom I began to love
    all on my own, I'm afraid now must be shared by me and
many others. Am I mistaken or has she become well known
    in my books? That's how it is – she is prostituted by means of
my talent. And I deserve it! For why did I publicly proclaim
    her beauty? My girl, through my own fault, has been made into
a saleable commodity. She gives pleasure with me acting as
    her pimp, the lover has been led in under my leadership and
her door opened by my hand.

    (Ovid 3.12.5–12)

But it isn't customary to hear poets as if they were legal witnesses;
    I had preferred weight to be lacking from my words too.

    (Ovid 3.12.19–20)

The prolific licence of poets knows no bounds and doesn't shackle
   itself to historical veracity. And my woman ought to have seemed to
have been falsely praised; now your credulity causes my injury.

(Ovid 3.12.41–44)

Discussion

The narrator here addresses the problem of love poetry in the public
domain. It is, he says, a vicious circle. His praise of his beloved has
provoked the interest of others and now he has to deal with the
consequence: his girlfriend is no longer his exclusively. This intolerable
situation, he fumes, is based on the ridiculous and naive reading habits
of his audience. Poets, he alleges, make up all sorts of ridiculous things
you aren't supposed to take literally. His praise of his *domina* was no
different in type to all those mythological stories you can read – you
would be a fool to take all that seriously.

Exercise

Now read the extract below and think again about how the author is
playing with the reader.

I know a certain woman who puts it about that she is Corinna[2].
   What wouldn't she give so that she could be?

(Ovid 2.17.29–30)

Discussion

You can see here how the Ovidian narrator enjoys blurring the
boundaries between text and life. Indeed, he points to an audience
that is liable to confuse art and life. This poem, unlike 3.12,
demonstrates, from the narrator's perspective, the positive rather than
the negative aspects of such confusion.

This interrogation of the boundaries between art and life may all have
been part of the expectations that a reader brought to the act of
reading elegiac poetry, a genre where the narrator bore the same
name as the real author and where, from our limited biographical
information, it seems that the age of the external poet was not
dissimilar to that of the wayward narrator in the text. All this may
have combined to encourage a response to reading elegy where the
line between text and reality became a little hazy, and perhaps part of
the success of elegy was in encouraging this fuzziness between art and

---

[2] 'Corinna' is the name of Ovid's *domina*.

life. The elegist, we might say, is promoting a self-serving image of notoriety. It is also possible that the elegist is deliberately mocking those who read naively and assume art and life coincide. If this is the case, the poet therefore seems to be conspiring with the more sophisticated segment of his reading audience in the derision of his less able readers.

Summary

Roman love elegy was a genre of poetry that in its finest form flourished for a period of twenty years or so during the time Octavius/Augustus was in charge of Rome. Like all ancient poetry, it was a sophisticated artistic product; it was written in a definite metrical form and with a high degree of conscious artistry and erudition. The initial impression we form of this type of poetry from the excerpts and whole poem that we have studied is likely to be that it must have been a fairly confrontational form of poetics in the climate of social conservatism and the return to traditional values promoted by Augustus. Indeed, the genre could be read as a sort of youthful counter-cultural movement whereby the young defiantly opposed the values being imposed on them by their parent culture.

However, we have also seen that this poetry can be interpreted in a very different fashion. It could be read as a caricature of wilful but misguided youthful behaviour, an adolescent carnival that eventually closes with the assumption of a more mature and reasoned perspective. We do not know, of course, exactly how an Augustan Roman audience responded to this form of poetry, but it is important to bear in mind that various different responses were possible.

Finally, in the last part of this section, we have taken a look at the conventions of ancient poetry and thought about some of the differences between our expectations of poetry and those of an ancient audience. It is important to bear in mind the importance of convention in ancient poetry and of sincerity as an effect rather than a principle of poetic composition. A poet like Ovid, as we have seen, can have a great deal of fun in playing with these conventions and toying with his readers.

5.5   Virgil's *Aeneid*

In the final section of the block we turn away from smaller-scale forms of poetry to the grandeur of epic poetry and look at perhaps the most famous piece of poetry ever written in Latin: Virgil's *Aeneid*.

If you have the time, you might like to do some optional reading here and look at the following:

- *OCCC* entry on 'epic'

Epic poetry

You have already studied the *Odyssey* and the *Iliad* in Block 1, so you have a good idea already of what epic poetry involves, and even before your study of Homer you probably had some idea of what 'epic' means. I imagine this was probably not poetry. 'Epic' to us conjures up an image of sweeping scale – we might think of something like a novel such as Tolstoy's *War and Peace* or a movie like *Ben Hur*. The meaning of epic for us of 'grand scale' has moved beyond the poetic form to which it originally applied.

In the realm of poetry, though, epic poetry refers to a long narrative poem that celebrates the deeds of one or more legendary heroes (such as Odysseus in the *Odyssey* or Achilles in the *Iliad*). These heroes are typically aided and/or thwarted by divine agents, and are also quite often part-divine themselves. The action of an epic poem frequently involves superhuman exploits on the battlefield, or voyages and eventful encounters with the weird and wonderful; quite often the action can also involve the founding of a nation, as a sort of quasi-divine justification for a race's pre-eminence.

The epics of Homer that you studied in Block 1 are sometimes called 'primary' epics – works that are thought to derive from an oral tradition; other examples are the Anglo-Saxon epic *Beowulf* (eighth century CE) and the Babylonian *Gilgamesh* (*c.*3000 BCE). Epic poems composed in a culture of literacy (such as Virgil's *Aeneid*) are often referred to as 'secondary' epics.

The form of epic: the hexameter

You will have considered the hexameter metre in your work earlier on the *Odyssey*. Ancient epic poetry was written in the hexameter metre, a metrical form divided into six units (called feet) of combinations of long and short vowels. There are two basic patterns for each 'foot': either a long syllable followed by two short syllables (called a 'dactyl') or two long syllables (called a 'spondee'). Either a dactyl or a spondee can be used in the first four feet; the fifth foot is almost always a dactyl and the last foot is either a spondee or a shortened form of a dactyl consisting of a long syllable followed by a short syllable. The end of a hexameter line almost always has a sound that can be summed up in the short phrase 'strawberry jam jar'; the whole line sounds like the following (which you encountered in the last section as the first line in an elegiac couplet):

> Down in a deep dark dell sat an old sow munchin' a beanstalk ...
>
> (Anon.)

When we read (or 'scan') the metre of a line of verse we write in the notation for the long and short syllables above the line of poetry. A long syllable is marked with the symbol ˉ and a short syllable with the symbol ˘.

So a spondee appears as ‾ ‾ and a dactyl appears as ‾ ˘ ˘; the divisions between the 'feet' are marked by slashes or vertical lines. If we 'scanned' the line above, we would end up with the following:

‾   ˘ ˘ / ‾   ‾ / ‾ ˘ ˘ / ‾   ‾ / ‾ ˘ ˘ / ‾   ‾

Down in a /deep dark/ dell sat an/ old sow/ munchin' a/ beanstalk ...

The possible variation in the first four feet of dactyls and spondees means that the metre can put across a wide variety of sound effects; using mostly spondees will lead to a very heavy, ponderous, sombre sounding rhythm, whereas the use of mostly dactyls will produce an effect of tripping along much more lightly. In Virgil's hands the hexameter reached an acclaimed peak of artistry summarised in Tennyson's verdict: 'Wielder of the stateliest measure ever moulded by the lips of man' (Tennyson, 'To Virgil', line 20). Tennyson wasn't quite so complimentary about Homer's use of the hexameter, however. Two of his imitation lines of Homer's verse read as follows:

These lame hexameters the strong-wing'd music of Homer!

When was a harsher sound ever heard, ye Muses, in England?

(Tennyson, 'In Quantity: On Translations of Homer', lines 1 and 3)

Exercise

To let you hear the rhythm and sound of Virgil's hexameters in their original Latin, we have recorded three excerpts from the *Aeneid* and their translations on CD4, Tracks 49–57. Listen to these recordings now before proceeding.

From Greece to Rome

Homer remained the epitome of epic poetry in the ancient world. As we have seen earlier in this part of the block, the great poets of the Augustan period reworked Greek poetic forms in their own distinctive way. We might say that for these poets the act of transplanting Greek poetry into a Roman context was a major creative challenge. Just as imperialistic ambition spread the Roman empire across the Mediterranean, so too were Rome's poets engaged in their own form of literary imperialism as they strove to build a Latin literary culture that rivalled the achievement of the ancient Greeks. Latin literature was engaged in a sort of Oedipal struggle with its Greek predecessor, and the earlier achievements of the Greeks were a constant barometer for the Romans of how to gauge their own success.

In all literary forms this was an immense challenge, but perhaps more so in the field of epic than anywhere else. Epic was acknowledged in the ancient world as being the highest form of literature. It was, therefore, a sort of battleground for a culture's artistic achievement. However, for Rome's poets, this was a very daunting battleground. Homer was *the* great poet of antiquity, the colossus of the ancient literary world. How could one even begin to match the achievement and reputation of such a figure? Could one out-Homer Homer?

If you have the time, you might like to do some optional reading here.

• *OCCC* entry on 'Virgil' (in particular, the introduction and the section on '*Aenied*')

Virgil

Virgil (whose full name was Publius Vergilius Maro; you will also see his name written as 'Vergil') was born in northern Italy in 70 BCE. At the time of his birth, this part of Italy was not part of Roman Italy but rather Cisalpine Gaul (Gaul on the Italian side of the Alps). He was not therefore born a Roman citizen (Cisalpine Gaul wasn't fully incorporated into Roman Italy until 42 BCE). Virgil doesn't appear to have been from a particularly wealthy background, but he does seem to have received a good liberal education and he ended up in the literary circle that formed around Maecenas (like Horace and Propertius).

It seems probable that Virgil's family also suffered deprivation during the turbulent times of the civil wars, with their land being confiscated to settle veteran troops. However, we should be careful not to assume this, as these details are heavily based on Virgil's poetry itself, which is not the most reliable medium for biographical details.

The *Aeneid* represents the culmination of Virgil's literary career. Before he turned to this epic work he had already composed the pastoral poems known as the *Eclogues* and a didactic poem on the countryside, the *Georgics* (see the *OCCC* entry on 'Virgil' for further details). Composition of the *Aeneid* took place from around 30 BCE onwards. The poem was near completion in 19 BCE when Virgil set off on a voyage to Greece; he fell ill soon into his trip and died a few days after returning to Italy. Before he died, the poet ordered the destruction of the poem, but his demands for the manuscript to be given to him so that he could throw it on the fire fell on deaf ears; Augustus himself stepped in to ensure that the poem was preserved and published. There are some surviving half-lines that Virgil never completed, but the poem we have is certainly a coherent whole and a polished piece of literary artistry – testimony to the painstaking care that its author took in its composition. Virgil is said to have written a line of verse in the morning and spent the rest of the day revising it, and to have compared his own process of writing to a mother-bear slowly licking her cubs into shape.

Virgil was not the first Latin author to write an epic poem. His most notable predecessor was Ennius (239 to 169 BCE). Ennius is a pivotal figure in the history of Latin literature: he first introduced the hexameter to Rome as the metre for an epic poem, his own *Annals*, which were written on the theme of Rome's history down to his own time. (Only fragments of the poem survive; you can read more about Ennius by looking up his entry in the *OCCC*.) By the time we reach the Augustan age, Ennius' poetry would have seemed rather dated and unsophisticated: its fit of Latin to the hexameter metre was rough by the standards of the Augustans and its heavy use of alliteration would have seemed a touch crude. With its aspirations to the creation of a poetics that would match the standards of the Greek world, the Augustan age was a time ripe for an epic in the modern style.

Virgil, the Aeneid *and the Augustan context*

As with Horace's lyric poetry and Roman love elegy, it is important to consider Virgil's *Aeneid* in the historical context from which it sprang: Augustan Rome. This particular poem presents the question of historical context perhaps more urgently than any other poetical work of the era. The exact nature of the relationship between Virgil and Augustus is often taken as a fundamental key to the understanding and interpretation of the poem. We certainly have some evidence that Augustus took a great deal of personal interest in the poem. He was, as we have just seen, personally responsible for the preservation of the poem, but we also learn from snatches of biography that he strongly urged the poet to send outlines or finished excerpts of the poem to him, and that Virgil, not long before his death, personally recited Books 2, 4 and 6 to Augustus and his close family relations.

Whatever its relation to Augustus, the *Aeneid* is clearly a poem concerned with national identity (like Livy's histories which you looked at earlier in this block). The story of Aeneas is the story of the myths that led to the foundation of the city of Rome. Aeneas, therefore, is in many ways the 'proto-Roman', and his story and behaviour thus take on a wider significance than just the deeds of a heroic individual. The poem is not just the story of Aeneas, but by means of the clever embedding within the narrative of prophesies, of scenes on works of art etc, the mythical tale of Aeneas is also set within a wider frame of a continuity of Roman history stretching down to the Augustan era itself. Myth and history are thus cleverly intertwined in such a way that Virgil's characterisation of Aeneas inevitably has something to say about what he thinks it means to be Roman in general.

This sort of interlinking of the past and the present was very much an Augustan concern. As we considered earlier, Augustus strove to situate his own position as princeps within a wider continuity of traditional Roman practices. He also made this connection with the past more explicit in some of the many building works that he sponsored. For instance, the decoration and layout of the Augustan forum expressly sets out to link the achievements of Augustus with those of the past notable figures of Roman history (you will be looking at this building complex in more detail in Block 5). A statue of Augustus in a chariot was the centrepiece, but on either side of the forum were lines of statues of great Romans of the past, and in two semi-circular apses there were two statue groups: one centred on Romulus, who faces on the other side Aeneas, flanked by the kings of Alba Longa and members of the Julian family.

This whole complex thus gave an impression of Augustus as the culmination of a successful Roman march through history. The presence of Aeneas among these Romans of the past is significant as Aeneas was traditionally the founder of the Julii, the family to which Julius Caesar belonged and of which Octavius had become a member through his adoption. The myth of Aeneas was thus very much central to Augustus' integration of himself into the very fabric of Roman history. Virgil's treatment of this myth also built the same sort of links between past and present that appear to have preoccupied Augustus. Thus, in Virgil's epic poem, although the action itself is set in the mythic past, narrative devices such as prophesy and *ekphrasis* (descriptions of works of art) help to blur a static timeline and allow the shadowy world of myth to share elbow space with near contemporary events. In Book 1 there is a prophesy from Jupiter of the future greatness of Rome; in Book 6, when Aeneas goes down to the underworld, he is shown by his father a parade of future Roman heroes that includes Augustus; in Book 8 the narrator describes scenes depicted on the shield of Aeneas which include the Battle of Actium. In this manner, the distinctions between history and myth are subtly elided and the present gains the seeming validation of being predestined.

The choice, then, of Aeneas as the principal character of the poem, the interweaving of myth and contemporary history and the inclusion of the princeps and his actions among the flashes of the future would all suggest that Augustus had good reason to want to preserve this poem. It seemed to embody a serious artistic celebration of his place in Roman history in a manner that was both restrained but pointed.

Themes and interpretation

As we have just noted above, one of the principle functions of the *Aeneid* is to serve as a foundation poem; that is, to place the Romans and their present situation in a sort of predestined cosmic ordering of events. The necessity of doing this was perhaps all the more imperative in the post-civil war context, as we considered earlier in the section on Horace's lyric poetry. There was an intense need to believe in the future and to put the chaos of the immediate past behind them. In this sense, the *Aeneid* is very much a poem of its time and it is not difficult to draw analogies between the trials and tribulations that the Trojans undergo, from the sack of their city to the start of the foundation of a new order in Italy, and the sufferings that the Romans had themselves gone through in the civil war period.

At the same time, it is also natural to draw parallels between Aeneas as the leader of this proto-Roman community and Augustus as the leader of contemporary Roman society. One of the themes of the *Aeneid* can be seen as a meditation on leadership and the qualities needed to lead a nation. During the course of the poem the reader can see in Aeneas a figure who develops from an action hero-type of figure, like Achilles (in essence, an effective killing machine whose central concern is with personal honour), into a community leader who has to rein in his own feelings and inclinations to serve the greater good of those who depend on him.

Throughout the poem, Aeneas is given the epithet *pius* ('pious' or 'dutiful'); the continual application of this term to him is highly suggestive of the qualities needed to be an effective leader. It indicates not only religious devotion and obedience, but also a sense of obligation to family and the wider community. The manner in which Aeneas struggles to live up to these expectations points to the qualities that this proto-Roman leader needed to succeed, but it is also perhaps a positive reflection of his contemporary equivalent, Augustus, whose very name embodied these qualities. If Aeneas is seen as the prototype, then Augustus can be seen as the finished model: the culmination of Roman history in the perfect Roman leader.

This might all seem to suggest that the *Aeneid* is a finely crafted piece of poetic propaganda, a commissioned piece of panegyric. Indeed, Servius, the writer of a fourth century CE commentary on Virgil's epic poem, quite clearly states his belief that the *Aeneid* was designed to praise Augustus. It is a tribute to Virgil's artistry, however, that the poem continues to provoke debate over the question of where the poet's sympathies lay and how this shaped the *Aeneid*. The fact that critics of this poem often use exactly the same passages to support opposite interpretations of the poem as a whole (the end of the poem, for instance, has been read as both a validation and a critique of Augustus) suggests the complex feelings that this epic evokes.

The opening of the *Aeneid*

For our study of the *Aeneid*, we will be reading the first few lines of the poem from Book 1 and then the whole of Book 4.

Exercise

Turn now to the opening lines of the poem (1.1–11) in Reading 3.30. (You may also like to listen to the reading of the first seven of these lines and their translation on CD4, Tracks 50 and 54.)

Jot down some notes on how these lines set out the theme of the poem and how they characterise the poem's principal hero, Aeneas.

Discussion

The *Aeneid* opens with the words: 'I sing of arms and of the man' ('*arma virumque cano*'). These words deliberately allude to both of Homer's great epic poems, the *Iliad* and the *Odyssey*: 'arms' recalls the martial theme of the *Iliad* and 'I sing of ... the man' deliberately echoes the opening of the *Odyssey*: 'Sing, Muse, of the man who ...'. These echoes would have been immediately apparent to an ancient audience and would have signalled the great scope and ambition of Virgil's work – a Roman epic poem to rival the great masterpieces of the Greek world. This is the story of a man who is in exile – a Trojan after the fall of Troy – fated to found a new kingdom in Italy. ('Lavinium' is the name of the first settlement that will be founded by the Trojan exile in Italy, in the area known in Roman times as Latium.) The introduction of the notion of 'fate' is important. Aeneas (the 'man' in question) has a destiny to follow, a mission that is preordained. The accomplishment of this mission will set in motion the process that will lead to the foundation of Rome. However, the introduction makes it clear that following his destiny will not be easy: he will suffer on sea and land during his travels to get to Italy, and after he gets there he will suffer in war (you can see again here how Aeneas' experience combines the trails of both Homer's epics: warfare and voyage). He suffers because of the anger and hostility of Juno. You will also have noticed that his suffering is despite his being 'a man famous for his piety'(line 10). The introduction ends with this apparent paradox, a righteous man hounded by the implacable anger of the queen of the gods.

Background to the *Aeneid*, Book 4

After the introductory paragraph, the narrative goes on to explain the reasons behind the hostility of Juno towards Aeneas. This concerns the city of Carthage: Juno is the patron goddess of the city and the Romans, the descendants of Aeneas, are destined to destroy this city completely in the series of conflicts known as the Punic Wars. Juno, therefore, wishes to launch a pre-emptive strike against the Trojan exiles to make sure this never happens.

As the poem opens, the Trojans are already seven years into their wanderings after escaping from the sack of Troy. At this point they are off the coast of Sicily and very near to their destination, Italy. However, Juno contrives for a storm to blow the Trojans off course and deposit them on the coast of North Africa, near Carthage. To make sure things go smoothly for Aeneas, Jupiter dispatches his messenger, Mercury, to instil in the Carthaginians goodwill towards the Trojan refugees shortly to appear in their midst. The Trojans are well received by the Carthaginians and Dido, in accordance with Jupiter's plan, but Venus (Aeneas' mother) decides to take out some extra insurance and has Cupid inflame Dido with love for Aeneas. Book 1 closes with the Trojans and Carthaginians feasting together. Dido – now smitten with love for Aeneas – requests him to tell his story from the sack of Troy to the present.

Books 2 and 3 are taken up with Aeneas' narrative to Dido and the Carthaginians in response to her request at the end of Book 1. In Book 2, Aeneas tells the dramatic tale of the fall of the city of Troy that culminates with his escape through the city carrying his father on his shoulders and leading his son by the hand. Book 3 consists of Aeneas' account of the first seven years of their wanderings since leaving Troy and prior to arriving at Carthage. During the course of these years, Aeneas and his men undergo a series of (mis)adventures as they move westwards, stopping off in Thrace, Delos and Crete as they try to work out with the aid (and hindrance) of cryptic prophecies where they are supposed to be going. Along the way they encounter monsters like the harpies, Scylla and Charybdis, and also run into other Trojan exiles such as Helenus, another son of Priam and Andromache, the widow of Hector. Finally, they land in Sicily where Aeneas' father, Anchises, dies. After they set off from Sicily, Juno contrives the storm that drives Aeneas and his companions on to the shores of North Africa. Book 3 ends with the conclusion of Aeneas' story to the Carthaginians.

The *Aeneid*, Book 4

In Book 4 we return to the 'real time' of the narrative, after Aeneas concludes his story (which has occupied the whole of Books 2 and 3). Let's now have a look in more depth at the *Aeneid*, Book 4. The story of Dido and Aeneas was one of the most widely-read episodes of Virgil's epic poem, even in antiquity. This love story has captured the imagination of readers ever since its composition and Dido is perhaps one of the few characters from Roman literature who has really fired the artistic sensibilities of later cultures.

Exercise

Read through the translation of Book 4 in Reading 3.30. As you read, I would like you to jot down some notes on the following issues:

- How are the main characters in this episode, Aeneas and Dido, portrayed? Do you find yourself feeling more sympathetic to one or the other? What do you think the narrative has to say about the quality of their leadership?

- Do you see any irony in the narrative of Book 4 given the historical enmity between Rome and Carthage?

- How do you think the narrative of Book 4 links to the sort of issues we have discussed so far with regard to Augustus' politics and Roman poetry of the period?

Discussion

There are a lot of things to consider here, so I have integrated my discussion of these questions into several different sections.

Judging Aeneas

Carthage represents a huge temptation for Aeneas. After seven years of wandering, the city state of Carthage rising before his eyes is like a dream come true. Here he is presented with an opportunity both for personal emotional fulfilment and security for his own followers. Can we really blame the Trojan leader for wanting to seize this chance? However, Aeneas also knows that this is not the place that destiny has appointed for him. Thus temptation and obligation are set at odds with one another.

Aeneas is certainly subject to divine manipulation in this episode, but we must also consider that such intervention reflects his natural inclinations: for example, the temptation to abandon the trials and sufferings of his mission and to settle for the immediate gratification of a future in Carthage with Dido. The attraction of Carthage for Aeneas is obvious and Virgil has not portrayed in Aeneas a hero who is beyond human frailty. The true hero is not an effortless superman but a human being who must overcome his limitations.

The confrontation between Aeneas with Dido (lines 296–396, 'But the queen – who can deceive a lover?...he nevertheless carried out the commands of the gods and went back to his ships.') demonstrates the potential price to be paid in emotional terms for valuing the bigger picture over one's own desires. It is easy from a romantic perspective to characterise Aeneas as a heartless imperialist, but Virgil also makes evident the conflict in Aeneas as he is faced with the choice of staying with Dido or pursuing his mission. Notice how the narrator inserts comments which show the reader that there is a price to be paid by Aeneas too. When Dido finishes her initial speech, Aeneas is described in line 332 as struggling 'to fight down the anguish in his heart'; he finishes his own first speech (lines 360–61) with the words: 'Do not go on causing distress to yourself and to me by these complaints. It is not by my own will that I still search for Italy'. At the end of the exchange, Aeneas is presented as tormented by the conflict between his duty and his love:

> But Aeneas was faithful to his duty. Much as he longed to soothe her and console her sorrow, to talk to her and take away her pain, with many a groan and with a heart shaken by his great love, he nevertheless carried out the commands of the gods and went back to his ships.
>
> (lines 393–96)

When Anna makes a final appeal to Aeneas on behalf of Dido, there is a famous simile of an oak battered by the winds hanging on resolutely in the face of mighty storms. This might seem to present an image of Aeneas as hard and intransigent, but it is worth recalling the end of this passage:

> ... just so the hero Aeneas was buffeted by all this pleading on this side and on that, and felt the pain deep in his mighty heart but his mind remained unmoved and the tears rolled in vain.
>
> (lines 447–49)

There is endless debate as to whether the tears in question are Aeneas' or Anna's (what do you think?), but clearly the resolution of Aeneas is portrayed as coming at the price of personal suffering.

One of the big issues in this book, you will have noticed, is human passion and its effects. The major protagonists in this love affair are both leaders of their communities and thus their emotions not only affect themselves but also those who are dependent on them. How Dido and Aeneas respond to their passion, and the effect their responses have on their respective communities, are of central importance in this book.

Book 4 is a trial for Aeneas: a test of his resolve and his commitment to his Roman future. Aeneas is perhaps not very inspiring as a character; certainly he does not have the same charisma as Homer's principal epic leads, Achilles and Odysseus. But we must also remember that Virgil is not interested in depicting an action hero; what he is trying to do is to build a portrait of a man who must overcome his own weaknesses and moments of doubt in order to be a responsible leader of his community. This perhaps does not make for the most interesting of characters but it is essential to the epic's view of human endeavour. What must a person overcome to do the right thing? What are the costs of one's mistakes to oneself and to others? What must a leader deny to himself for the sake of his community?

The emotional exchange between Dido and Aeneas highlights the tough decisions that a leader must make. Once Aeneas is prompted, he chooses one form of devotion over another. He chooses to embrace the destiny of Rome rather than his personal happiness; the narrative makes it clear that his choice is not a decision that affects just himself. The message of Jupiter that Mercury repeats to Aeneas stresses to the Trojan leader that personal indulgence will rob both his son and his descendants of their proper glory. Aeneas chooses to love his destiny, not Dido. He puts his community before himself. Note the contrast between the dejection of Aeneas and the delighted reaction of the Trojans (lines 279–95, 'But the sight of him left Aeneas dumb and senseless ... They were delighted to receive their orders and carried them out immediately') to the news they are going to leave. The decision for Aeneas is not an easy one and he pays a price as well as Dido. (It is interesting to note that the Latin word for Rome, *Roma*, is an anagram of the Latin word for love, *amor*; we could say that this book is about how love ought to be spelled.) The foundation of Rome is not without cost both for those who will become Rome and those who are the incidental and accidental victims of history's progress. Destiny has its price; the question is whether it is worth paying.

Judging Dido

Dido is the Queen of Carthage. As such, it would have been easy for Virgil to characterise her in a wholly negative way, as the leader of a city traditionally hostile to Rome and its interests. However, notably Virgil does not do this and Dido emerges from the *Aeneid* as perhaps the most sympathetic character in the poem.

In Book 1 of the epic, Dido is shown as a strong and charismatic leader. She too is an exile and is intent on building a new secure future for her people (there are obvious parallels here between Dido and Aeneas and between the Carthaginians and Trojans). At this stage, Dido is clearly ahead of the game: she is in a situation (building a city for her people) that Aeneas can still only dream of. Ironically, it is the arrival of the Trojans that sends everything haywire. How then does everything go wrong, and what is the extent of Dido's culpability in this?

Does Book 4 pass a moral judgement on Dido? You will have seen how at the beginning of the book Dido is wracked with a sense of guilt as her feelings for Aeneas grow. She believes that she owes an obligation to her past husband (murdered by her brother, an event that precipitated Dido's own exile and her founding of Carthage) and that it would be morally wrong for her to form another attachment. This notion of life-long commitment to one man was, in fact, a cultural ideal of early Rome. Such a woman was called a *univira* and Dido is thus presented initially as embodying a Roman ideal of behaviour. This form of behaviour was certainly not a norm in the Augustan period, but we must remember that Augustus was very much concerned with promoting traditional values. Dido might seem a rather curious embodiment for these values, but perhaps what happens to her is a judgement on her failure to live up to this ideal.

Various circumstances work to change Dido's mind; there is, of course, the passion that has been breathed into her through the agency of Venus; there is also the advice of her sister, Anna, who sees in Aeneas and the Trojans the opportunity for the Carthaginians to make an alliance that will ensure their safety and prosperity in a potentially hostile environment. Thus we can see in Dido's increasing attachment to Aeneas a combination of motivations. Her passion appears to be the prime motivation, but her decision can also be justified on the grounds of the interests of her people. There is also the question of to what extent Dido herself is responsible for her own feelings. It is easy to view her as the innocent victim, a pawn in the divine rivalry between Venus and Juno and the plan of destiny that Jupiter safeguards. You will notice at the very end of the book that Dido is described as 'dying not by the decree of Fate or by her own deserts but pitiably and before her time' (lines 696–97). This would seem to suggest that the poet presents Dido's death as undeserved and not a necessary part of the divine plan.

However, it would also appear that there are points in the fourth book where culpability *is* suggested. There is the question not only of her breaking her bond to her former husband, but also her attitude towards her relationship with Aeneas. Again, there is divine involvement here. Venus and Juno contrive the 'marriage' between Dido and Aeneas, but whether this is a 'real' marriage is one of the big questions of Book 4. What's your opinion? You may have noticed that Dido's response to the 'cave incident' is portrayed in a very negative way:

> From now on Dido gave no thought to appearance or her good name and no longer kept her love as a secret in her own heart, but called it marriage, using the word to cover her guilt.
> (lines 170–72)

This seems to be a very damning indictment of Dido's behaviour and suggests that passion has overcome her better judgement.

Her involvement with Aeneas also stirs up trouble among the neighbouring peoples. Iarbas, in particular, is offended and it becomes clear that Dido's refusal to marry before was an effective strategy for playing her rivals off against each other (we might compare her actions here with the statesmanship of England's Elizabeth I). With an open attachment to Aeneas in place, the consequences are potentially ruinous if this relationship does not work out.

One of the great set pieces of Book 4 is the confrontation between Dido and Aeneas after the Trojan leader has resolved to leave. Here again it would have been easy for Virgil to present this argument as clear-cut in Aeneas' favour, but he does not really do so. As you read through this confrontation, I'm sure you found a great deal of strength in Dido's argument. She offered Aeneas and the Trojans hospitality; a debt has been incurred; she could be forgiven for thinking that the relationship between them was more than casual; her alliance with him has put her and her city in danger from others; she has compromised her own moral values for him. All of this is quite compelling and it would take a rather hard-headed reader to deny the force of Dido's argument and not to feel some sympathy with her position.

You might however have noticed a gender bias in the *Aeneid* that counts against Dido: for instance, on the divine level, where Jupiter represents a reasoned divine providence whereas Juno stands for the inexplicable, the unexpected and the irrational. This bias is also evident on the human level. It is Dido, the woman, who succumbs most heavily to passion and who cannot break free of it. Her very gender, the narrative presupposes, compromises her. When Mercury appears to Aeneas in a dream he emphasises this point in the famous misogynistic comment he passes on to Aeneas: 'Women are unstable creatures, always changing' (lines 569–70). Dido's violent reaction to Aeneas' departure and her curse on Aeneas and his descendants (lines 586–629, 'The queen saw from her high tower the first light whitening

... Let there be war between the nations and between their sons for ever') would seem to reinforce this negative stereotyping of women as the irrational agents of destructive forces. (It also serves, of course, as a mythical reason for the hostility between Carthage and Rome.)

The narrative on Dido is confusing and complicated and in this it effectively mirrors the complexity of human feelings and the various pressures of diverse obligations. If Dido has a tragic flaw, it is in her susceptibility to passion, her need to love and to be loved, a surely understandable human impulse. At one level the narrative seems to excuse her of any responsibility by stressing the role of divine agents in bringing this about, but at the same time one must consider (as we did in the case of Aeneas) that such divine figures are also in a sense personifications of human feelings and experience. The passion that is contrived in Dido by these divine agents can also be seen as a quality that resides in *her* and that will emerge in the right circumstances.

We saw above how the narrative appears to vindicate Aeneas as a leader by stressing how he sets aside personal emotional attachments in favour of the interests of the Trojan community. I'm sure you will have noticed, however, that at several points the narrative in Book 4 stresses how ruinous Dido's attachment to Aeneas is to the Carthaginian community. The narrator draws attention to the fact that Dido's increasing passion is directly proportionate to a decrease in the activity of fortifying her city: 'All the work that had been started ... all stood idle' (lines 88–89). This was the very activity – the industry of the Carthaginians in building their city – that Aeneas had so admired when he first arrived in Carthage in Book 1 (not in your course material). There he exclaims: 'How fortunate they are, their walls are already rising' (Aeneid 1.437).

In the Iarbas episode, you may also have picked up on the hostility which the relationship between Dido and Aeneas stirs up among the Carthaginians' potentially hostile neighbours. The inception of this relationship puts Carthage under threat and its failure could spell disaster.

At the very end of the book we read how the news of Dido's suicide has an effect on her city as though it were being sacked by enemy invaders:

> It was as though the enemy were within the gates and the whole of Carthage or old Tyre were falling with flames raging and rolling over the roofs of men and gods.
> (lines 669–71)

These passages make it clear how the behaviour of a leader affects the greater good of the community. As Dido surrenders to the passion that consumes her, Carthage and its citizens lose their zeal and energy; as Dido dies, the city is metaphorically in its death throes too.

I would say there are multiple viewpoints built into the *Aeneid* and multiple demands on our sympathies as readers. Issues are often not black and white. Characters who might easily have been characterised as melodramatic villains tend not to be and their dark, violent sides are often tinged with hints of human warmth and feeling. Characters whose passionate emotions lead to their ruin are not dismissed with high-handed moral judgement, but their suffering is finely and sympathetically narrated. Those who put others before themselves are not mindless slaves to duty and obligation, but have to battle with their own emotions and feelings. There are many grey areas in the poem, areas where the poem invites the reader to weigh competing viewpoints against each other and where judgement on whether a certain person has done the right thing is not easily resolved. This sort of complexity and ambivalence gives the poem great depth and ensures that questions of interpretation cannot be fixed with any certainty. As the poem also clearly blurs the distance between mythic past and contemporary events, it also serves to project all these difficult questions and issues into the present Roman climate and its immediate past.

The irony of the situation

One aspect of Book 4 that would have been striking to a Roman reader (but perhaps tends to pass a modern reader by) is the great irony that pervades the events of this book. Carthage was the great enemy of Rome and the relationship between Aeneas (whose descendants will found Rome) and Dido (the queen of Carthage) must have seemed a preposterous mismatch, contrived by the divine agents in the poem for their own ends (Juno is trying to protect Carthage and Venus to protect Aeneas). The relationship between the two is quite contrary both to the path of destiny that is set out in the *Aeneid* and also to the events of history with which a Roman reader would be familiar.

The ridiculousness of this situation is made most apparent in the scene (lines 259–76, 'As soon as his winged feet touched the roof of a Carthaginian hut ... You owe him the land of Rome and the kingdom of Italy') where Jupiter (provoked by the prayer of Iarbas) dispatches Mercury to confront Aeneas with his failure to pursue his destiny. Here Mercury encounters Aeneas dressed in Carthaginian style, helping with the building of Carthage. This must have been quite a shocking picture for a Roman reader: Aeneas, the founder of the Roman race, is actually helping to build the city of Rome's mortal enemy; these are the very walls that Aeneas' own descendants will later destroy. Aeneas, of course, does not have the benefit of historical hindsight; he does not know that this city is the last place that he should be thinking of building his future in. This sort of historical irony helps to highlight the inappropriate nature of the relationship between Dido and Aeneas.

Book 4 in the context of Augustan Rome

Virgil's *Aeneid*, like the other poetic examples we have looked at in this part of the block, is intricately connected to the historical context out of which it arose. Naturally, it is possible to appreciate this poem, or Horace's lyric poetry or Roman love elegy without a detailed knowledge of the Augustan period, but such a knowledge does add an extra dimension to our appreciation. As we have seen, the Augustan period is presented very much as a new beginning for Rome, albeit one founded on tradition. In this way, the *Aeneid* was a work very much of its time.

The *Aeneid* is a complex work and its many ambivalences have been used to demonstrate that the poem is both pro- and anti-Augustan. But to see the work as either propaganda or a diatribe is a crude reduction of the poem's artistic presentation. Virgil himself must have felt a certain ambivalence towards Augustus and the new order. After all, his own family probably suffered through confiscations instigated by Octavius (as did Horace's family, and Propertius appears to have lost relatives in the civil conflicts that Octavius was in part responsible for). But, then again, Virgil did owe his own material wellbeing to the new order.

The *Aeneid* is a tale of balancing loss and achievement and this balance could be seen to be epitomised in the character of Aeneas. He makes mistakes, he and others pay the price, but he does what he thinks he has to do in order to secure the future of those dependent on him. He may be a frail hero, but doesn't this make his achievements all the more admirable? Loss, suffering and self-sacrifice are all presented as foundations for future success and security. It is an austere message, but perhaps not a surprising one coming from the context of a society emerging from generations of bloody civil conflict. In this manner, the image of Aeneas emerging from the ruins of Troy with his father on his back and leading his son by his hand (an image that formed one of the central statue groups in the Augustan forum, as you will see in

Block 5, Sections 1.3 and 1.4; Readings Book 2, Reading 5.3; and Plate 61 of the Illustrations Book) is a potent one. Aeneas is burdened by the past but is giving the future a helping hand. Is this not precisely the image that Augustus wanted to present of himself and the restoration of Rome? This city, too, was burdened by the past, but Augustus, a man like Aeneas his ancestor, and equally distinguished by his piety, was helping to give it a bright future.

The intricacy of Virgil's depiction, however, meant that his poem could always be read with different emphases (think again about how the message of Roman love elegy might be processed in quite different ways according to the sensibility of the reader). A reader of the *Aeneid* might choose to emphasise the cost, loss and suffering entailed in Rome's imperial mission; from this perspective, Aeneas is not a positive role model and his reflection on his contemporary equivalent, Augustus, will be a minus rather than a plus. Augustus would emerge not as saviour but as the latest in a long line of imperialist oppressors. There is certainly plenty of scope for 'pessimistic' readings of the *Aeneid*, but we do not know the intentions of the author and we would not be bound by them even if we did. We should, however, consider our own involvement in history and how it might affect our interpretations. The question is not just one of how context affects an author, but also how your own reading of a work is similarly qualified by the cultural and historical context in which you are reading it.

References

Ancient sources

Augustus, *Res Gestae* 8 and 34, T. Fear (trans.), Latin text from http://www.thelatinlibrary.com/resgestae.html (accessed 1 March 2006).

Coleridge, *Ovidian Elegiac Metre*, from http://www.cornellcollege.edu/classical_studies/meters.shtml (accessed 1 March 2006).

Horace, *Odes* 3.6, in W.G. Shepherd (trans.) (1963) *Horace: The Complete Odes and Epodes*, London: Penguin, pp.138–140.

Ovid, *Amores* 1.9.1; 1.15.1–6; 2.1.2; 2.4.1–6; 2.17.1–3; 3.12.5–12; 3.12.19–20; 3.12.41–44; 2.17.29–30, T. Fear (trans.).

Tennyson, 'In Quantity: On Translations of Homer', from http://whitewolf.newcastle.edu.au/words/authors/T/TennysonAlfred/verse/enocharden/inquantity.html, lines 1 and 3 (accessed 1 March 2006).

Tibullus 1.6.85–86 and 2.4.1–4, T. Fear (trans.).

Propertius 1.1.1–7; 1.6.29–30; 1.12.19–20; 2.1.57–58; 2.15.29–30; 2.22A.17–18; 2.24.5–7; 3.5.1–2; 3.8.23–24; 3.24.14–20 and 3.25.1–2, T. Fear (trans.).

Propertius 2.7, in V. Katz (trans.) (2004) *The Complete Elegies of Sextus Propertius*, Princeton University Press, p.105.

Part 6   Conclusion to Block 3

During this block you have studied a wide range of sources and evidence in your investigation of historical themes. The sources and your analytical study of them have been very varied, but they are all held together by their relevance to the study of Rome in the last few centuries BCE. In extremely general terms, the central themes of this block have been politics, competition, the creation of history, and the relationships between society and literature. But is it possible to also consider the sources and the historical themes as part of a broader process of cultural development? And if so, what kind of a narrative of cultural development can be written?

Exercise

Read Beard and Crawford, Chapter Two, 'The Cultural Horizons of the Aristocracy', pp.12–24. There should be much in this chapter that is by now familiar because they are discussing the same period, and some of the same sources, that you have been studying in this block. Reading Beard and Crawford's account of how culture developed in the late republic will consolidate what you have learned throughout this block. As you read, summarise their argument.

Discussion

The central argument of the chapter is an attempt to outline a process of cultural development in the Roman republic. Beard and Crawford emphasise the fundamental role of Greek culture within Roman culture. They identify a three-stage process starting with a translation of Greek works, which leads to the adaptation of Greek originals, which in turn stimulates a cultural 'take-off' and the emergence of a distinctive Roman culture. Nevertheless, Beard and Crawford state on p.15 that this is only a *schematic* framework, an aid to making historical sense of the sources. They are, in essence, describing a theoretical process that accounts for the changes they have observed; their discussion picks out examples of sources that they can fit into their historical process of cultural development. It seems that their process is one that points to a flowering of culture in the late republic and Augustan period. Can you imagine where other sources and evidence that you have studied can be fitted into this process?

Exercise

As a rather topsy-turvy final exercise in consolidation and revision, I would like you now to read Chapter One of Beard and Crawford, 'The Nature of the Problem, pp.1–11. (You have read some of this before.) As you read this time, summarise first the methodological problems outlined on pp.1–4, and secondly the descriptive framework on pp.4–11.

RLR

Discussion

Beard and Crawford have written what they describe on p.4 as an 'analytical description' of the collapse of the republic. They have picked out significant episodes or situations and fitted them into a process of historical change. As with the process of cultural development outlined in Chapter Two, their 'analytical description' is open to criticism and modification. Here we should be asking questions such as: does their theoretical model fit the facts? Is there some relevant area that they are not taking into account? Or, put another way, is their description too selective in the sources and evidence it uses? (There is no mention of the rapid physical development of the city of Rome as the context of the political and social conflicts, for example.) Is there a significant element of the collapse that their process does not take into account? (Have they paid sufficient attention to personal ambition and greed?) By questioning what you read in this way, you are applying what you have learned and considering whether the account you have read reinforces or challenges your own understanding of the period you have been studying.

I hope that reading these initial two chapters of Beard and Crawford at the end of the block has helped to refresh your thoughts about large-scale cultural and political developments in the late Roman republic. Beard and Crawford are well aware, as they make clear in their methodological introduction (pp.1–4), that there are no simple and clear answers or complete explanations. What is more, the analyses they provide are difficult to reconcile: the process outlined in Chapter Two is seen as a positive cultural flowering, whereas Chapter One analyses a downwards spiral of political conflict. The Roman republican period was a rich and complex mixture of diverse processes. Their exploration is a continual process of critical investigation, interpretation and debating.

Appendix   Timeline: The Roman republic

517 BCE	Traditional date of founding of the republic
*c.*280 BCE	Death of Cornelius Scipio Barbatus
264–241 BCE	The First Punic War
*c.*250–150 BCE	Life of Seianti Hanunia Tlesnasa
241 BCE	Sicily becomes the first overseas Roman province
238 BCE	Sardinia becomes a Roman province
234–149 BCE	Life of Cato
227 BCE	Corsica becomes a Roman province
221 BCE	Death of L.Caecilius Metellus
218–201 BCE	The Second Punic War against the Carthaginians
216 BCE	Battle of Cannae
*c.*180 BCE	Death of Publius Cornelius Scipio, son of Publius
197 BCE	Rome gained two new provinces in Spain (see p.20)
168 BCE	Rome defeats King Persius of Macedonia at the Battle of Pydna
*c.*167 BCE	Death of Lucius Cornelius Scipio, son of Lucius
*c.*166–133	Life of Tiberius Gracchus
*c.*157–86	Life of Marius
156–121 BCE	Life of Gaius Gracchus
149–146 BCE	Third Punic War
146 BCE	Destruction of Carthage by the Romans
	Africa becomes a Roman province
	Corinth destroyed by the Romans
	Macedonia and Achaea become Roman provinces
*c.*138–78 BCE	Life of Sulla
135–132 BCE	Slave revolt in Sicily
*c.*130 BCE	Death of Gnaeus Cornelius Scipio
129 BCE	Asia becomes a province
106–48 BCE	Life of Gaius Pompeius Magnus (Pompey)
106–43 BCE	Life of Cicero
105 BCE	Battle of Arausio
100–44 BCE	Life of Gaius Julius Caesar
*c.*90–30 BCE	Life of Diodorus Siculus
92 BCE	Prosecution of Publius Rutilius Rufus
91–88 BCE	Social War between Rome and her allies
88 BCE	Mithridates VI, King of Pontus, 'liberates' Asia and orders the massacre of all the Romans
87–84 BCE	Sulla's campaigns in the Greek east
83–79 BCE	Sulla dictator
73–71 BCE	Slave revolt in Italy led by Spartacus
70–19 BCE	Life of Publius Vergilius Maro (Virgil)

69 BCE	Funeral of Julia
65–8 BCE	Life of Quintus Horatius Flaccus (Horace)
63 BCE	Cicero consul
63 BCE–CE 14	Life of Octavian (Augustus)
62–31 BCE	Triumviral period
c.54–2 BCE	Life of Sextus Propertius
49 BCE	Caesar starts a civil war by crossing the Rubicon
44 BCE	Caesar murdered
43 BCE–CE 17	Life of Publius Ovidius Naso (Ovid)
35 BCE	Sallust dies
31 BCE	Octavian wins the battle of Actium becoming sole ruler of the Roman world
27 BCE	Octavian receives the title Augustus
CE c.23–79	Life of Pliny the Elder
CE c.40–c.102	Life of Martial
CE c.45–120	Life of Plutarch
CE c.100–c.160	Life of Appian
CE 138–161	Antoninus Pius emperor